PREPARE (& SURVIVE!)

The New Zealand guide to getting yourself through emergency events

STEPHEN BARNETT

Published in 2025 by David Bateman Ltd,
Unit 2/5 Workspace Drive, Hobsonville,
Auckland 0618, New Zealand
www.batemanbooks.co.nz

ISBN 978-1-77689-145-0

A catalogue record for this book is available from the National Library of New Zealand.

Book design: Cheryl Smith, Macarn Design
Images: Sources shown on page 185
Printed in China by Everbest Printing Co. Ltd

CONTENTS

INTRODUCTION 6

PART 1 — DISRUPTION TO EMERGENCY 15
Earthquakes 20
Floods 28
Landslides 33
Storms 37
Tsunamis 46
Volcanic activity 51
Wildfires 57
Other emergency scenarios 60

PART 2 — PREPARING AND SURVIVING 65
Before you start 65
A quick guide to preparedness and action 72
Making plans 84
Emergency supply kits and grab bags 94
First aid essentials 103
Shelter 107
Food and water 111
Utilities 124

Emergency toilets 134
Emergency communications 147
Transport during an emergency 156

AFTERMATH 160

EMERGENCY INFORMATION AND CONTACTS 174

ACKNOWLEDGEMENTS AND CREDITS 183

INDEX 186

HOW TO USE THIS BOOK

Part One profiles various emergency risks with suggested responses before, during and after the event. Part Two presents a detailed 'how-to guide' for securing or replacing the needs of shelter, power and so forth. At the end of the book is grouped information on emergency contacts and resources.

DISCLAIMER

The information contained in this book has been gathered from a variety of reputable sources and is, to the best of the Author's and the Publisher's knowledge, the most accurate and up-to-date information available at this time. The Author and the Publisher assume no responsibility for the outcome of any situation that results from following the guidelines specified in this book. The information provided in this book should be used in conjunction with any official recommendations from government and/or safety officials, and not as a replacement.

INTRODUCTION

'BE PREPARED!'

On hearing the old Scout motto for the first time, someone asked Scouting founder Robert Baden-Powell, 'Prepared for what?' To which Baden-Powell replied, 'Why, for any old thing.' In *Scouting for Boys*, Baden-Powell wrote that to Be Prepared means 'you are always in a state of readiness in mind and body to do your duty'.

IF A NATURAL DISASTER OR ANOTHER EMERGENCY EVENT HAPPENED RIGHT NOW, HOW READY WOULD YOU BE? HOW WOULD YOU FARE? AND FOR HOW LONG?

Natural emergencies such as storms, earthquakes, floods, volcanic activity and wildfires can strike unexpectedly, putting lives at risk and causing widespread disruption and destruction. As can other 'man-made' crises such as infrastructure failure or cyber-attacks. In today's world we are increasingly reliant on complex energy, transport and logistic systems to maintain our lifestyles; great while these systems are working but if they suffer a major disruption then normal life can hit a big bump in the road.

It's often not until a crisis occurs involving such systems that we realise the extent of our dependence on and vulnerability to their interconnectedness and to the digital world that makes it all happen. If a major problem occurs, you're talking goodbye — briefly if we're lucky — to ATMs, the internet, mobile phones, computers, the electricity necessary for the running of our households, and hello to empty shelves at our local supermarkets.

We can predict few, if any, disruptions and emergencies and when they do happen, they can be at a level that will have a significant impact on your daily life. Your first and best defence, for yourself and your family, your household, is to be ready, as much as possible, for anything.

Lack of preparation can stem from a perception that the risk of an event of this scale happening is extremely low, or we consider the time horizon too distant, or there's an unwillingness to commit funds to preparing. Sometimes we don't even realise the threat exists, but the unexpected can happen at any moment.

AND THINGS DO GO WRONG

Take the world banking system. Judged to be 'too big to fail', in 2008 it did just that, precipitating a global financial crisis that saw many people lose their jobs and many economies plunged into recession. Closer to home, in 2017, when the fuel pipeline to Auckland from the oil refinery in Northland was broken, the lack of a secondary fuel supply line to the city, and, in particular, for jet fuel to Auckland's airport, came as a surprise to many, not least to those in government. Yet the need for such an important back-up should have been obvious.

At the beginning of the following decade, with no expectation or warning — and even less preparation for it — the Covid-19 pandemic brought about millions of deaths worldwide and a huge social and financial cost.

The Canterbury earthquakes of 2010 and 2011; the tragedy of White Island's eruption in 2019; 2023's historic rainfalls and cyclones; 2024's global IT breakdown all revealed further gaps in our awareness of, and preparation for, the risks around us and how to deal with their fallout.

The following extracts from the report by Peter Boshier, the Chief Ombudsman, on the 2023 weather events titled *Insights and Observations: The Chief Ombudsman's report on extreme weather events 2023* provide a record of what we're up against:

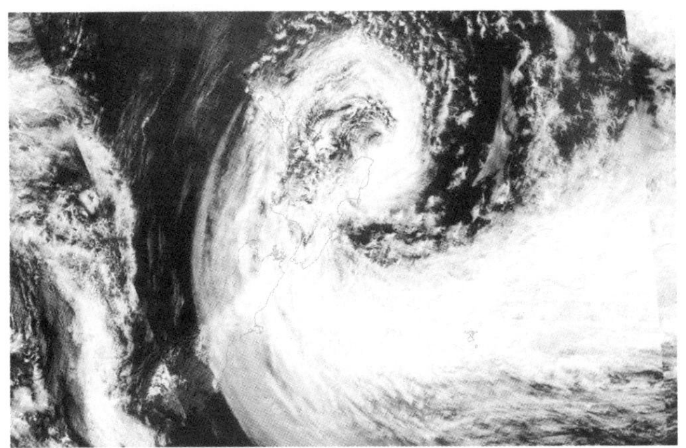

A composite satellite image of Cyclone Gabriel from February 2023. The cyclone's effect across the North Island was devastating, its extreme lashing winds and rain causing flooding, landslides and storm surge. Thousands of people were left without power, many lost their homes and possessions and there was huge damage to road networks and other infrastructure.

The start of 2023 saw New Zealand struck by a series of extreme weather events which seriously impacted much of the North Island. In early January, Cyclone Hale caused severe flooding in areas such as Te Tai Tokerau | Northland, Tāmaki Makaurau | Auckland, Waikato and Tairāwhiti | East Coast. States of emergency were put in place, reflecting the savageness of Hale's impact. Shortly after, the worst floods in Auckland's history occurred during Auckland Anniversary Weekend. More than a month's worth of rain fell in a single day on the Auckland region, leading to widespread flooding, land slips and property damage. That intense rainfall extended from Northland to the Waikato and Bay of Plenty regions where it caused more severe flooding and dangerous river conditions.

. . .

While the country was still reeling from these events, Cyclone Gabrielle struck between 12 and 16 February, with devastating effect. Gabrielle left a catastrophic trail of destruction across the North Island, and overwhelmed regions already ravaged by Hale. Homes and businesses were razed. Lifeline infrastructure was severely compromised, and critical road networks were destroyed. Sadly, four people lost their lives to the Auckland Anniversary Weekend floods and 11 more to Cyclone Gabrielle. Thousands of other people were left isolated and displaced.

. . .

It is easy to underestimate just how isolated some towns, communities and regions were as a result of the North Island weather events. In areas like the East Coast and Northland, Cyclone Gabrielle washed away roads and bridges that in some places were the only access routes in and out of communities. Across Northland, damage to roads meant damage to critical services built alongside them, like power and telecommunications. In other regions, flooding and slips disabled substations and telecommunication towers, resulting in lost phone and internet connections. Places like Tokomaru Bay, Hokianga, Piha, Wairoa and Eskdale, to name but a few, were completely isolated from the rest of the country – in some cases for weeks.

. . .

These events highlighted how vital infrastructure is, and how vulnerable it is to worsening extreme weather.

. . .

Some of the communities I visited told me they quickly realised they would need to be self-sufficient, not just for a few days, but in some cases for weeks and months . . . they knew they must rely on themselves.

. . .

Extreme weather-related events will have a profound and enduring impact on individuals, communities, regions and, indeed, our country as a whole. They should no longer be considered novel. They are part of New Zealand's reality.

Whether it's a natural hazard or another emergency event, the outcome comes as a profound shock to our lives, necessitating our having to suddenly deal with the loss of our homes and jobs, shortages of items in our shops, no power or transport fuel or no access to our bank accounts. It is crucial, therefore, that we act ahead of time to prepare and mitigate the effect of such events. Being prepared and then being capable of smart choices during the event and the aftermath is something every household should work towards.

In an emergency, emergency services will be on the scene, but they won't be able to reach everyone immediately. You could be stuck at home without basic services such as electricity, gas, drinking water, flushing toilets and phones, for days or even weeks. How you get through will depend on your initial actions and not those of emergency services and authorities. The safety and survival of yourself, your family and those around you will depend on what you do.

There's little doubt that climate change may trigger more frequent and more forceful natural hazard events, particularly those relating to flooding and storms, while demands on infrastructure along with the vulnerability of our increasing reliance on the internet and digitised systems will only add to potential emergencies.

The purpose of this book is to help you build resilience through preparation and adaptability, to decrease your vulnerability to things beyond your control and to improve your ability to adapt to changing circumstances.

BE PREPARED, BECOME RESILIENT, SURVIVE

While it's not possible to anticipate every emergency, you can put plans in place to make sure your whole family is prepared. A good way to begin is to imagine a major disruption event and think about how long you could survive self-contained. Think about how much you depend on an ever-present supply of food, water, energy, of having a place to lay your head, reliable transport and having your waste removed and sanitary needs met. These are all things we've come to expect, but what happens if they are taken away?

ASK A FEW 'WHAT-IFS' AND THEN START TO PUT TOGETHER A PLAN BEFORE AN EMERGENCY OCCURS.

Being prepared for any emergency is as simple as planning ahead. To some, it may all sound a little like 'the boy who cried wolf' because, in most instances, the disruption is minor and the lights *will* come back on after a few hours, but it has to be remembered that the wolf *did* turn up in the end. Having a stash of extra food, water and back-ups of things you may need such as torches, a battery radio and a first aid kit is only sensible.

Think about just what impact various events could have on your daily life and go from there. The first step should be establishing an emergency store of food and water, this isn't difficult and will greatly help your confidence before and in the wake of an emergency. It doesn't need to take up a great deal of space or cost a fortune — a couple of cardboard boxes stored at the back of a wardrobe will make a big difference should the time come. *Do it.* Treat the task as another form of insurance. *Be prepared.*

PART 1

DISRUPTION TO EMERGENCY

– BEING PREPARED FOR ANYTHING

In New Zealand, the risks of natural disasters and other hazards are very real. Earthquakes, floods, landslides, severe storms, tsunamis, volcanic activity, as well as 'man-made' emergencies, can happen at any time and often without warning — all of them capable of seriously disrupting our lives, or worse.

In a major, widespread emergency — such as a high-magnitude earthquake — emergency services may be unable to reach you immediately or even soon after the event. If this happens, it will be essential to your wellbeing, even survival, that you are able to last at least a few days (perhaps even weeks) on your own without the assistance of emergency services, without access to groceries from the store, without electricity or without the sewerage system being operable.

EMERGENCIES CAN HAPPEN ANYTIME, ANYWHERE, AND OFTEN WITHOUT WARNING.

The National Emergency Management Agency (NEMA) is New Zealand's leading agency for emergency preparedness, survival and recovery. Its website explains the 4 most important aspects of preparedness:

1	Knowing how to keep safe before, during and after different types of emergencies.
2	Creating and practising a household emergency plan.
3	Putting together a household kit of emergency survival items, keeping water and food supplies refreshed as necessary.
4	Having a grab bag packed with essential items in case you have to leave your home or workplace in a hurry.

THE FIRST AND BEST DEFENCE IS TO BE READY. THIS WILL GREATLY IMPROVE THE ODDS OF SURVIVING.

Statistically, disruptions and emergencies are most likely to be caused by natural events such as storms, flooding and earthquakes. The following table describes some of Aotearoa New Zealand's worst emergencies since the mid-1800s:

YEAR	TYPE	LOCATION	DESCRIPTION
1846	Landslide	Te Rapa, Lake Taupō	Worst landslide in New Zealand's history.
1855	Earthquake	Wairarapa	Magnitude 8.2
1863	Flooding	Central Otago	Blizzard and flood.
1886	Volcanic	Mount Tarawera	Destroyed the Pink and White Terraces.
1918	Health Crisis	Nationwide	Influenza virus, October–December 1918.
1931	Earthquake	Napier	Official death toll of 256, with 2 marked unaccounted for. Magnitude 7.8. New Zealand's deadliest natural disaster.
1936	Weather	North Island	The Great Storm of February 1936 – cyclone.
1953	Volcanic	Tangiwai	Lahar from the Mt Ruapehu crater lake destroyed a rail bridge, sending overnight train into river.
1968	Earthquake	Inangahua, West Coast	Magnitude 7.1
1968	Weather	North Island	Cyclone Giselle – recorded as the worst storm in New Zealand's history.
1979	Landslide	Dunedin	69 houses destroyed.
1988	Weather	East Coast of North Island	Cyclone Bola – one of the most damaging cyclones to hit New Zealand.
2009	Health Crisis	Nationwide	Swine flu infected 3,175 people and resulted in 19 deaths.
2011	Earthquake	Christchurch	Magnitude 6.2 – 185 deaths.
2016	Earthquake	Kaikōura	Magnitude 7.8 – 2 deaths.

YEAR	TYPE	LOCATION	DESCRIPTION
2017	Wildfire	Port Hills, Canterbury	A devastating fire that burned more than 1600 hectares of land on the Port Hills in February 2017.
2019	Volcanic	Whakaari / White Island	Explosive eruption causing 22 deaths and severe injuries to many others.
2020	Health Crisis	Nationwide	Covid-19 infected over a million people leading to nationwide lockdowns in late March 2020 and August 2021 and an Auckland-wide lockdown in August 2020.
2021	Flooding	Auckland	Heavy rainfall caused extensive flooding and slips in western Auckland resulting in 1 death.
2023	Flooding	Northern North Island	From 27 January to 2 February, catastrophic floods occurred in the Auckland, Northland and Waikato regions which resulted in states of emergency, with Auckland being the worst affected. NIWA reported a record breaking 150 millimetres (5.9 in) of rainfall across the city in a span of 3 hours.
2023	Weather	North Island	Cyclone Gabrielle struck the North Island from 12 February to 15 February, resulting in significant damage and flooding, and a national state of emergency being declared for the third time in NZ's history.
2024	Wildfire	Port Hills, Canterbury	A wildfire broke out on 14 February and lasted until 6 March. 700 hectares of land was burned, and a state of emergency was declared, with evacuations of residential properties.

There's little reason to expect that natural emergencies will decline. In fact, the effect of global climate change is likely to increase both the frequency and severity of many natural hazard events.

We need then to look at what we can do, individually and as communities, to prepare for such emergency events, to take precautions to lessen their impact while they are unfolding and to increase our resilience for the next time.

EARTHQUAKES

Aotearoa New Zealand straddles the boundary of 2 tectonic plates: the Pacific Plate to the east and the Australian Plate to the west. These plates are constantly colliding with huge force, causing them to grind over, under or alongside each other. As the brittle crust of the plates gives way under the pressure, a fault ruptures and an earthquake is unleashed. Around 20,000 earthquakes are recorded in and around New Zealand every year, of which 150–200 are strong enough to be felt.

Usually occurring without warning, the bigger quakes can cause massive damage to our towns, cities and rural areas. Secondary impacts such as tsunamis, infrastructure failure and landslides can become emergencies themselves.

Topping the list of potential sources of catastrophe-sized earthquakes is the Hikurangi Subduction Zone where a high magnitude earthquake and resulting tsunami could see tens of thousands dead and injured and hundreds of thousands of people displaced.

And then there's the Alpine Fault. Running 600 kilometres along the spine of the South Island, the Alpine Fault is overdue for a large earthquake with a high probability of rupturing in the next 50 years. Research estimates such an earthquake would be around magnitude 8. Each time it has ruptured in the past, the Alpine Fault has also moved vertically, creating and lifting the Southern Alps in the process.

WHAT TO DO BEFORE AN EARTHQUAKE

- Help earthquake-proof your home by securing items that could fall and hurt you in an earthquake to a wall (e.g., bookcases).
- Review your insurance regularly. Having insurance cover for your home and contents is important to help you get back on your feet if you suffer damage in any emergency. Use your mobile phone to regularly video the contents of your home and the externals of the property as a record for insurance purposes.

- Make a plan to help you get through staying in place and also for if you have to evacuate.
- Identify safe spaces within your home, school, work and other places you often visit in case you suddenly need to DROP, COVER and HOLD during an earthquake. Safe places should be those close to you, no more than a few steps away, to avoid injury from flying debris:

- Under a strong table. Hold on to the table legs to keep it from moving away from you.
- Away from windows that can shatter and cause injury. And away from tall furniture that can fall on you. Protect your head and neck with your arms.
- Not in a doorway: in most homes, doorways are no stronger than any other part of a house and a swinging door can cause more injury.

WHAT TO DO DURING AN EARTHQUAKE

Earthquakes can be very frightening, but you need to try not to panic. Once you have found yourself a safe space, stay there until the earthquake stops shaking. If you are inside, do not run outside, or you risk getting hit by falling bricks and glass.

While the earthquake is happening, the correct action to take is to **DROP**, **COVER** and **HOLD**.

When the shaking starts, quickly find some cover and DROP, COVER and HOLD until the earthquake is over.

DROP down onto your hands and knees. This stops you from being knocked over but allows you to move around if needed.

COVER your head and neck – or your entire body if possible – under a sturdy table or desk (if it is within a few steps of you). If there is no shelter nearby, cover your head and neck with your arms and hands. If you cannot do that, shelter against an interior wall away from windows, bookcases and other hazards. Covering your body makes you a smaller target for falling and flying objects and protects your head, neck and vital organs.

HOLD on to your shelter (or your position to protect your head and neck) until the shaking stops. If the shaking shifts your shelter around, move with it.

DROP, COVER AND HOLD – what to do

- **If you're outside** – Move away from buildings, trees, streetlights and power lines. Then **Drop**, **Cover** and **Hold**.
- **If you're in an elevator** – **Drop**, **Cover** and **Hold**. When the shaking stops, try and get out at the nearest floor – only if it is safe to do so.
- **If you're driving** – Pull over to a clear location – away from any trees and power lines, and not under a bridge – and come to a complete stop. Wait there with your seatbelt fastened until the shaking stops. Once the shaking stops, proceed with caution and avoid bridges or ramps as they may have been damaged.

- **If you're in bed** – **Stay**, **Cover** and **Hold**. Stay in bed and pull the sheets and blankets over you. You are less likely to be injured if you stay in bed. Cover your head and neck with your pillow. Hold on until the shaking stops.
- **If you have a mobility impairment or use a cane** – **Drop**, **Cover** and **Hold** or **Sit**, **Cover** and **Hold**. Get down as low as you can or sit on a chair or bed. Cover your head and neck with both hands. Keep your cane near you so you can use it when the shaking stops. Hold on until the shaking stops.
- **If you use a walker or wheelchair** – **Lock**, **Cover** and **Hold**. Lock your wheels and get as low as possible. Bend over and cover your head and neck as best you can. Hold on until the shaking stops.
- **If you are near the coast** – If the earthquake is 'Long or Strong' then 'Get Gone' and move quickly away from a possible tsunami. During the shaking, first protect yourself from the earthquake by **Dropping**, **Covering** and **Holding**. When the shaking is over, if the earthquake has lasted longer than a minute or is strong enough to make it difficult to stand, move quickly to the nearest high ground or as far inland as you can get and out of tsunami evacuation zones.

Do not run outside or you risk getting hit by falling debris and glass. Should you become **trapped under debris,** try not to move or kick up dust as it could choke you. Use a piece of your clothing to cover your mouth. Shouting out may cause you to inhale dust. Instead make other kinds of noise, if you can, to alert help – tap on a hard object or on a pipe so that rescuers can locate you. Use a whistle if you have one. Try to protect your eyes from concrete dust.

WHAT TO DO AFTER AN EARTHQUAKE

- Expect more shaking from aftershocks. Each time you feel shaking: **Drop**, **Cover** and **Hold**. More shaking can happen minutes, days, weeks, months and even years following an earthquake.
- If you are in a tsunami zone and the earthquake was long or strong (long means the shaking lasts more than 1 minute, strong means it is difficult to stand up), evacuate immediately to higher ground or as far inland as possible after the shaking stops.
- Get first aid if necessary.
- Assess your home or workplace for any damage. If the building appears unsafe get everyone out. Use the stairs, not an elevator, and when outside, watch out for fallen power lines or broken gas lines. Stay out of damaged areas.
- Look for and extinguish any small fires if it is safe to do so. Fire is a significant hazard following earthquakes.
- Listen to the radio for updated emergency information and any further instructions.
- Do not overload phone lines with non-emergency calls. If possible, use text messaging or social media instead.
- Help people who require special assistance – infants, elderly people, those without transportation, families who may need additional help, people with disabilities and the people who care for them.
- Turn off water and electricity. If you see sparks, broken wires or evidence of electrical-system damage, turn off the electricity main switch, which will be located on the main switchboard, if it is safe to do so. Turn off water at boundary – pipes may be broken inside buildings, and this can cause unseen water damage.

- If you smell gas or hear a blowing or hissing noise, turn off the gas if you can or get advice. Open a window. Get everyone out quickly and call your gas supplier — get their advice on whether or not you should turn the gas off at the main valve, as once it's turned off, restoring the supply will require a professional tradesperson to do so.
- If you can, put on protective clothing that covers your arms and legs and wear sturdy footwear to protect yourself from injury by broken objects.

If your property is damaged

Do not do anything that puts your safety at risk or causes more damage to your property. Contact your insurance company as soon as possible. If you rent your property, contact your landlord and your contents insurance company. Take photos of any damage. It will help speed up assessments of your claims.

Damaged buildings in Christchurch following the 2011 earthquake in Canterbury. Christchurch's central city and eastern suburbs were badly affected, with damage to buildings and infrastructure already weakened by an earthquake only months previously. While the initial 2011 earthquake only lasted some 10 seconds, the damage was severe because of the location and shallowness of the earthquake's focus. Nearly 200 people lost their lives.

FLOODS

Floods are New Zealand's number 1 hazard, often causing major damage, loss of utilities and loss of life. You may not be immediately aware of a flooding threat, however, as flooding may result from rainfall some distance away; heavy rain in the upper part of a catchment can lead to flooding far downstream long after the rain event.

PUT YOUR SAFETY FIRST. DON'T TAKE ANY CHANCES. ACT QUICKLY IF YOU SEE RISING WATER.

FLOODS

WHAT TO DO BEFORE A FLOOD

Getting ready before a flood happens will help reduce damage to your home or business and help you survive. Find out what the flood risk is in your area. Ask your local council about evacuation plans and public alerts. Follow advice from MetService. Make a plan and practise your evacuation route to get to higher ground.

IF FLOODING IS A POSSIBILITY

- **Stay informed** by listening to the radio or follow your local Civil Defence Emergency Management Group online.
- **Stay put** in your home or office if you can without risk. If you feel unsafe or see rising flood-water, evacuate to higher ground. Do not wait for official warnings.
- **Have a waterproof flashlight** to use if power goes out and it's dark, as well as for signalling for help.
- **Be prepared to evacuate** by keeping your grab bag nearby. Listen to emergency services, your local council and Civil Defence. Follow any instructions about evacuation in your area. Self-evacuate to higher ground if you see rising water or if you feel unsafe.
- **Move your pets** to a safe place. If you must leave, take your pets with you if there is time.
- **Turn off utilities** (water, electricity and gas) if advised to.
- **Move valuable and dangerous items** as high above the floor as possible. This includes electrical equipment and chemicals. Use watertight containers to store important items.

- **Lift household items** – as high above floor level as possible. Lift curtains, rugs and bedding off the floor.
- **Check on your neighbours** – anyone who may need your help ahead of a flood.

WHAT TO DO DURING A FLOOD

- **Put safety first** – Don't take any chances. Act quickly if you see rising water. Get to higher ground. Floods and flash floods can happen quickly
- **Never try to walk, swim or drive through flood-water** – Many flood deaths are vehicle related – caused by driving through flood-water or attempting to move a stranded vehicle. As little as 30 centimetres of water can cause you to lose control of your vehicle. The depth of the water is not always obvious, stopping you from seeing hazards such as potholes or washouts. Rapidly rising water may stall the engine or engulf the vehicle, and you and the vehicle can be quickly swept away by rapidly rising water. Attempting to walk through flood-water – unless absolutely necessary – is not recommended. Children, especially, may be at risk of being swept away. Flood-water can often also contain dangerous debris that is not easily visible.
- **Always assume that flood-water is contaminated** – Contaminated flood-water can make you ill. Make sure you wash any parts of your body that have had contact with flood-water. Wash your clothes and other items that have been in contact with flood-water.
- **Listen to the radio** – As broadcast radio is one of our most resilient communication channels, it is the primary channel for public information in a large-scale emergency response. You can also check the websites of your local council and your local Civil

Defence Emergency Management Group. Follow any instructions from local Civil Defence authorities or emergency services regarding an evacuation of your area.

- **Stay up to date** — Make sure you're aware of the latest weather information from MetService. Pay special attention to Watches and Warnings.
- **Keep a waterproof flashlight close by** — This will be important to help find your way and to signal for help. Use the torch on your mobile phone if you don't have a handheld torch.

WHAT TO DO AFTER A FLOOD

- **Returning home** — Only return home after your local council, Civil Defence and emergency services have advised that it is safe to do so; it may not be safe to return home even after flood-waters have receded.
- **Look before you step** — After a flood, the ground and floors may be slippery or covered with debris, including broken bottles and nails.
- **Dangerous chemicals and biohazards** — These can enter flood-water from the ground surface, septic tanks and sewage systems. This can contaminate drinking water, land and any surfaces it touches.
- **Throw away contaminated food and water** — Anything that has come into contact with flood-water, including foodstuffs stored in containers. These may have been damaged and their seals compromised. Canned foods should be okay to consume so long as cans are not damaged.
- **Avoid** — Don't drink or prepare food with tap water until you are certain it is not contaminated. Follow any 'boil water' instructions from your local authorities.

- **Stay away from damaged areas** – Your presence might hamper rescue, obstruct other emergency operations and put you at further risk.

If your home has been affected, it is important to clean and dry it and everything inside it. Protect yourself – wear gloves, protective goggles and boots while you do this. Flood-water may contain sewage and other hazardous materials that can contaminate your home. Contact your utility supplier if your gas, electricity or phone lines have been affected by water or debris.

LANDSLIDES

Landslides and debris flows are essentially rivers of rocks, earth, and other debris saturated with water. They develop when water rapidly accumulates in the ground, during heavy rainfall or snowmelt. They can occur without any obvious trigger but are most commonly set off by heavy rainfall and earthquakes. Activities such as mining, construction and the removal of trees and vegetation can also cause or increase the likelihood of landslides.

Possible causes also include unstable land on steep roadside cuttings and leaking water pipes. Landslides may also dam-up rivers and if these fail, be responsible for flooding downstream.

WHAT TO DO BEFORE A LANDSLIDE

Some areas are at a higher risk of landslides — including areas with existing old landslides, steep slopes, drainage channels on steep slopes, stream and riverbanks, or coastal cliffs. Find out from your council if they have information on landslide hazards and risk, if there have been landslides in your area before, and where they might occur again. If you have a slope on your property, check drains are clear and adequate, and that retaining walls are in good condition. Be aware that landslides on another property could affect you, if you are in the path of a landslide runout.

- Noticing small changes can alert you to an increased threat of a landslide. Be aware of the warning signs of unstable ground: small slips, and rockfalls; subsidence at the bottom of slopes; doors and window frames that start to stick, or gaps developing around them; outside fixtures like steps, decks and verandas moving or tilting away from your house; new cracks or bulges on the ground, road or footpath; trees, retaining walls, fences and telephone poles that start to tilt.
- Watch the patterns of storm water drainage on slopes near your home, and especially the places where runoff water converges, increasing flow over soil-covered slopes.
- Landslides can occur without any warning. Be aware of the potential for landslides, particularly in the weeks after potential trigger events, such as heavy rainfall, earthquakes and previous landslides.

WHAT TO DO DURING A LANDSLIDE

Act quickly. If you suspect that a landslide is occurring, or is about to occur in your area:

- Evacuate immediately if it is safe to do so. Seeking higher ground outside the path of the landslide is your best protection. The side of your house furthest from the landslide is likely to be the safest location within your property.
- Be aware of sinkholes and underground washouts.
- Take your pets with you if you can do so without endangering yourself.
- Alert your neighbours, they may not be aware of the potential hazard.
- Stay up to date with the latest weather information from MetService. Pay special attention to heavy rain warnings. Short bursts of heavy rain may be particularly dangerous, capable of triggering landslides, especially if the ground is already saturated after longer periods of wet weather.

WHAT TO DO AFTER A LANDSLIDE

Following a landslide, stay away from the area as further landslides may occur. Stay away until the area has been properly inspected and authorities give the all-clear.

- After heavy rainfall, don't drive unless absolutely necessary and stay away from areas where landslides have occurred previously.
- Be especially alert when driving. Embankments along roadsides are particularly susceptible to landslides. Watch the road for collapsed areas, mud, fallen rocks and other indications of a possible debris flow.
- Look for broken utility lines (electricity, telephone)

and report them to the appropriate authorities. Reporting potential hazards will get the utilities turned off as quickly as possible, preventing further hazard and injury.

- Take photos of any damage to your home and land, as well as your contents; having photos will help speed up assessments of your insurance claim.

STORMS

Storms occur in a variety of forms — thunderstorms and snowstorms, for example. They're low-pressure systems that bring with them strong winds, often with heavy rain, hail, lightning, tornadoes, heavy swells, coastal inundation and storm surges. All of which pose threats to people and their homes and businesses.

The most damaging are **tropical cyclones** (called hurricanes or typhoons in the northern hemisphere). These are large storms with sustained wind-speeds of at least 60 kilometres per hour to as much as 120 kilometres per hour or more. While these tropical cyclones are no longer classified as such when they meet the cooler sea temperatures around New Zealand, they still remain dangerous, capable of major damage to rural and urban areas.

Tornadoes sometimes occur during thunderstorms, their narrow, violently rotating wind columns extending downwards to the ground from the base of the thunderstorm. While generally small in New Zealand, they can still cause severe localised damage and threaten lives. They are usually around a few tens of metres wide, have tracks a few kilometres long and exist for just a few minutes.

Know the warning signs for tornadoes:

- A long, continuous roar or rumble, or a fast-approaching cloud of debris, which could be funnel shaped.
- If you see a tornado funnel nearby, take shelter immediately. Shelter in a basement if you have one or an inside room – stay away from windows and exterior doors. Get under sturdy furniture and cover yourself with a mattress or blanket.
- If caught outside, get away from trees if you can. Lie down flat in a nearby gully, ditch or low spot and protect your head.
- If in a car, get out of the car immediately and look for a safe place to shelter. Do not try to outrun a tornado or get under your vehicle for shelter.

WHAT TO DO BEFORE A SEVERE STORM

- Practise your emergency plan, make up grab bags for your household and store emergency supplies.
- Stay up to date with the latest weather information from MetService, paying attention to weather Watches and Warnings.
- Listen to advice provided by your local Civil Defence Emergency Management Group and emergency services and follow any instructions. However, emergency warnings may not always be issued or received in time due to infrastructure failure. Use your judgement and evacuate if you feel unsafe.
- Postpone outdoor activities if a storm is imminent.
- If you hear distant thunder or see a flash of lightning, get indoors immediately.
- If you see a tornado funnel nearby, take shelter immediately.
- Identify a safe location in your home for household members to gather during a thunderstorm. This should be a place away from windows, skylights or glass doors, which can be broken by strong winds or hail and cause damage or injury.
- Keep materials at hand for repairing windows, such as tarpaulins, boards and duct tape.
- Bring inside or tie down anything that can be broken or picked up by strong winds, such as outdoor furniture. If you have a trampoline, turn it upside down to minimise the surface area exposed.
- Clear debris and leaves from external drains and gutters to prevent overflow or water damage in heavy rain.
- Pull curtains and blinds over windows. This can prevent injuries caused by flying glass if the window breaks.

- Close all interior and external doors. Closed doors will help prevent damaging winds from entering rooms.
- Take extreme care with items that may conduct electricity if your home is struck by lightning.
- Using electric lights is safe, but it is recommended you unplug appliances and avoid using the telephone or any other electrical appliance, especially television sets.
- Turn off air conditioners and heat pumps, which can be overloaded by power surges from lightning.
- If you live in an old house with metal plumbing, avoid using bathtubs, water taps and sinks as these may conduct electricity.
- Use battery-powered radios and water from your emergency supplies.
- Keep a torch, battery-powered lantern and spare batteries handy.

TREES NEAR POWER LINES

Trees and power lines are not a good mix. In windy conditions and during storms, tree branches and other vegetation can blow on to power lines leaving them either hanging low or bringing them down to the ground. If you come across low-hanging or downed power lines, keep people and animals well clear and report it to your local power lines company. Keeping trees clear of power lines, and not planting new vegetation near them, keeps us all safe and helps keep the power on. When overgrown, trees can interfere with power lines, cause outages when branches or even whole trees bring down the power lines and make it difficult for utility crews to restore power. It's said that trees and branches interfering with power lines cause a quarter of all power cuts.

SEVERE WEATHER OUTLOOKS, WATCHES AND WARNINGS

Severe Weather Outlooks, Watches and Warnings are issued by MetService and are available on radio, television, the MetService website and the MetService mobile app.

Typically, MetService will issue advice 6 days out from potential severe weather by way of a **Severe Weather Outlook**. This applies to large areas of rain, wind and snow. The Outlook is a 'heads up' that, although severe weather is coming, there is some uncertainty about what might happen and where.

As an event gets closer, MetService can be more specific about severe weather timing, location and intensity. MetService will issue a **Severe Weather Watch** (with colour-code Yellow) or a **Severe Weather Warning** (with colour-code Orange or Red, depending on the severity of the event).

- **Severe Weather Watch – Yellow**: Bad weather is coming or getting closer. Watches are issued as required for events expected in the next 48–72 hours, or for events expected in the next 24 hours where uncertainty is high.
- **Severe Weather Warning – Orange**: MetService are confident about what is going to happen. They warn about when and where warning criteria will be reached, and the impacts of this weather will be significant.
- **Severe Weather Warning – Red**: This event is extreme and is among the worst that we get – it will have substantial impacts, and it is possible that a lot of people will be affected. The situation may be similar to Cyclone Gita in February 2018, the Fiordland/Southland floods of February 2020, the Canterbury flood of May 2021, the Buller flood of July 2021 or Cyclone Gabrielle in 2023.

Warnings regarding thunderstorms are different as thunderstorms form incredibly quickly and are less predictable. At most, a 'heads up' **Thunderstorm Outlook** is issued up to 36 hours before the event (covering 'today' and 'tomorrow'), and a **Severe Thunderstorm Watch** is typically issued within 6–12 hours of the event. **Severe Thunderstorm Warnings** are issued once a severe thunderstorm is observed on weather radar and provide information on where the storm will move in the next 60 minutes.

WHAT TO DO DURING A SEVERE STORM

- Stay inside: Don't walk around outside. Don't drive unless absolutely necessary.
- Close all exterior and interior doors and windows. Pull curtains and blinds over windows to help prevent injuries caused by flying glass if windows break.
- Stay informed: Listen to the radio or follow your local Civil Defence Emergency Management Group online. Follow the instructions of Civil Defence and emergency services.
- Avoid bathtubs, water taps and sinks: Metal pipes and plumbing can conduct electricity if struck by lightning. Use the water from your emergency supplies instead.
- Unplug small appliances that may be affected or damaged by electrical power surges. If you lose power, unplug major appliances. This will reduce the power surge and possible damage when power is restored. A surge protector is a single-use device – it will only be effective once, replace it ASAP after use.
- Check on your neighbours and anyone who might need your help. Check for injuries and get first aid if necessary.

If caught in a **snowstorm**, do all you can to keep as warm as possible. The goal should be to retain heat: having a 'space blanket' (also known as a Mylar blanket) in your emergency supplies will increase your chances of surviving as the foil material will reflect heat back towards your body. Keep a space blanket in your car as well for emergencies. Be aware of the effects severe cold can have on people – such as slurred speech – and act immediately. It's hard to get warm if you're wet, so try to stay as dry as possible and change into dry clothes if you have them.

If you are caught outside during a **lightning storm** and you hear thunder or see a flash of light, get indoors immediately. Being inside a sturdy structure is safest: avoid gazebos, rain or picnic shelters and other isolated structures, these offer little protection from large hail, can be struck by lightning and are often poorly anchored and subject to being uprooted and blown around in strong winds.

- If you are boating, fishing or swimming at the time of a lightning storm, get to land, get off the beach and find shelter immediately.
- If you are in a car, pull safely onto the shoulder and stop, making sure you are away from any trees or other tall objects that can fall on the vehicle. Turn on your hazard lights to alert other drivers that you have stopped. Stay in the vehicle with your windows closed. In a vehicle you are safer from lightning than out in the open. Avoid contact with metal or other conducting surfaces inside and outside the vehicle to reduce your chance of being shocked.
- If you are in the bush, find an area protected by a low clump of trees. Never stand beneath a single large tree in the open. Be aware of the potential for flooding in low-lying areas.

- If you're not near a suitable shelter, as a last resort find a low-lying, open place away from trees, poles or metal objects. Make sure the place you pick is not subject to flooding. If you are physically able to, crouch low to the ground, on the balls of your feet. Place your hands on your knees and put your head between your knees. Minimise your body's surface area and minimise your contact with the ground. Lightning currents often enter a victim through the ground rather than by a direct overhead strike.

Avoid places and objects such as:

- Tall structures or elevated areas such as towers, tall trees or hilltops, as lightning normally strikes the tallest objects in the area.
- Open or exposed spaces such as exposed sheds or construction sites. Move to a location beneath a solid roof and avoid openings such as windows or doors.
- Any electrically conductive objects such as metal fences, clothes lines, power lines and telephone lines.
- Objects in metallic contact with the ground. Machinery such as tractors are often struck by lightning, so don't seek shelter under these.

WHAT TO DO AFTER A SEVERE STORM

If there is surface flooding in your area and you see rising water, do not wait for official warnings. Head for higher ground and stay away from flood-waters.

- Never try to walk, play, swim or drive in flood-water
- If it is safe to do so, check in on neighbours, friends and family who may have been affected, and offer support.

- Stay away from damaged areas. Your presence might hamper rescue and other emergency operations and put you at further risk from the residual effects of floods, such as contaminated water, crumbled roads, landslides, mudflows and other hazards.
- Be careful if having to walk flooded streets. Fast-moving murky water can hide the presence of debris and holes.

IF POWER LINES HAVE FALLEN OR THERE'S IMMINENT DANGER:

- All fallen lines should be treated as live. Call 111 and keep yourself, other people and animals at least 10 metres away from the fallen line. Stay away from trees or cars that are touching fallen lines.
- Do not try to rescue people or animals trapped by lines until they have been made safe by a professional.
- If a power line falls onto a car, it may still be live. Do not try to rescue people from cars trapped by fallen lines. If you are the one inside a car trapped by a fallen line, stay there and phone for help. Wait for a professional to make sure the line has been made safe. If you are in danger, however, and must exit the car, jump clear of the car keeping your feet together when you land. **Do not touch the ground and the car at the same time.** Once clear of the vehicle, shuffle away, keeping your feet together until you are at least 10 metres away. Keep away from pools of water as these may also conduct electricity.

TSUNAMIS

Tsunamis are sea waves generated by earthquakes, volcanic eruptions or landslides. In deep water, tsunamis have long wave lengths and short wave heights. The deeper the water the faster the tsunami. In the deep ocean, tsunamis can move as fast as a jet plane and can cross entire oceans in less than a day. As the waves enter shallow water near land, they slow and the waves increase significantly in height.

Tsunami damage is caused by the force exerted by flowing water onto structures, and by run-up of the wave onto land, which causes flooding and carries debris with it. Tsunamis can also generate dangerous current speeds that can be hard for vessels to navigate. The tsunami waves can move a long way onto shore very quickly.

Most often, a tsunami has more than 1 wave. It may not be safe to be near low-lying coastal areas for up to 24 hours after the initial wave as much larger waves often follow the initial one. After the first wave reaches land its drawback trough pulls the water back a long distance and there may be only minutes before the next big wave hits.

While tsunamis are rare, they can have a deadly impact: the earthquake in Japan in 2011, known as the Great East Japan Earthquake and measuring magnitude 9, set off a massive tsunami that devastated many areas along the country's Pacific coast, and 18,000 people died as a result.

WHAT TO DO BEFORE A TSUNAMI

All of New Zealand's coast is at risk of tsunami. Your local Civil Defence Emergency Management Group has tsunami evacuation zone maps and advice on where to go whether you are at home, at work or out and about. Work out a route for getting yourself and your family to higher ground.

Know where the nearest high ground is, and how you will reach it, particularly if you live in a low-lying coastal area. Plan to get as high and as far inland as you can.

Discuss the evacuation route with your household. For a local-source tsunami, which could arrive in minutes, there won't be time for an official warning and it's important to recognise the natural warning signs and act quickly. Do not wait for official warnings. If you are in a tsunami zone and experience any of the following, take immediate action:

- Feel a strong earthquake that makes it hard to stand or a long earthquake that lasts more than a minute.
- See a sudden rise or fall in sea level.
- Hear loud or unusual noises from the sea.

If an earthquake is **LONG OR STRONG, GET GONE**. As soon as the shaking stops, move immediately to the nearest high ground or as far inland as you can out of the tsunami evacuation zone. The earthquake is your only warning. Do not wait for an official tsunami warning. Do not return until you get an official all-clear message from Civil Defence.

If an earthquake occurs in the Pacific Islands or further away, we may not feel it. If there is a tsunami threat to New Zealand, a national warning will be issued by the National Emergency Management Agency (NEMA). Tsunami warnings are published on the National Emergency Management Agency's website and will also be broadcast on radio and television.

The National Emergency Management Agency is the official tsunami warning agency for New Zealand. NEMA will issue a tsunami warning to Civil Defence Emergency Groups, emergency services, the media and the public.

Immediately follow the advice of any emergency warning. Do not wait for more messages before you act.

WHAT TO DO DURING A TSUNAMI OR WHEN A TSUNAMI WARNING HAS BEEN ISSUED

If you feel an earthquake that is Long or Strong, Get Gone. The earthquake itself is your only warning that a tsunami is possible. If you are in a tsunami zone, evacuate immediately to higher ground or as far inland as possible after the shaking stops.

DROP, COVER and **HOLD** during an earthquake. As soon as the shaking stops, move immediately to the nearest high ground or as far inland as you can get, out of tsunami evacuation zones. Even if you can't get out of your evacuation zone, go as far or as high as you can. Every metre makes a difference.

- Walk, run or cycle to reduce the chances of getting stuck in traffic congestion. Don't wait in your car if there is a traffic jam and a tsunami is on its way, you may end up being swept away while you're waiting. Get out of your car and run to higher ground.
- Take your pets with you only if this will not delay you. Don't spend time looking for them and if you are not at home, don't return to get them.
- Do not return to your home until you get an official all-clear message from Civil Defence.

WHAT TO DO AFTER A TSUNAMI

Keep away from the evacuation zones until they are considered safe.

- Return home only when you are told it is safe to do so by Civil Defence.
- Listen to the radio or follow your Civil Defence Emergency Management Group online for more information and instructions.

- If there was an earthquake, expect more shaking. More earthquake shaking could generate another tsunami. Be prepared to evacuate.
- Stay away from coastal water, tidal estuaries, rivers and streams for at least 24 hours after any tsunami or tsunami warning. Even small waves create dangerous currents.
- Avoid areas impacted by the tsunami. You might hamper rescue and other emergency operations and be at further risk from the residual effects of tsunami flooding.
- Help others if you can.
- If your property is damaged, do not do anything that puts your safety at risk or causes more damage to your property. Contact your insurance company as soon as possible.

IF YOU'RE BY THE COAST AND THE EARTHQUAKE IS LONG OR STRONG, GET GONE.

VOLCANIC ACTIVITY

Volcanism in New Zealand has been responsible for many of the country's geographical features, especially in the North Island and the country's outlying islands.

While the country's volcanism dates back to before the Zealandia microcontinent drifted away from Gondwana 60–130 million years ago, activity continues today with minor eruptions occurring every few years. This recent activity is primarily due to the country's position on the boundary between the Indo-Australian and Pacific Plates, which are a part of the Pacific Ring of Fire (also known as the Circum-Pacific Belt – a path along the Pacific Ocean characterised by active volcanoes and frequent earthquakes), and in particular the subduction zone where the Pacific Plate dives under the Indo-Australian Plate.

New Zealand has seen many large explosive eruptions during the last 2 million years, including several of super volcano size. Taupō's most recent major eruption took place around AD 232. It ejected some 120 cubic kilometres of material, and it is believed that the eruption column was 50 kilometres high. The resulting ash turned the sky red many thousands of miles away.

A major eruption of recent times was that of Mt Tarawera in June 1886. Ash and debris were spewed over 16,000 square kilometres, destroying the Pink and White Terraces and 3 Māori villages, claiming the lives of perhaps 120 people.

The Tangiwai disaster of December 1953 occurred when the Tangiwai railway bridge across the Whangaehu River was swept away by a lahar (mudflow) from Mt Ruapehu's crater lake just before a passenger train was about to cross it. 151 people died when the train was unable to stop in time and it plunged into the river.

More recently was the eruption of the Whakaari/White Island volcano in December 2019. A group of 47 visitors were on the island when the volcano erupted and 22 people died, either in the explosion or from injuries sustained. A further 25 people suffered serious injuries, with the majority needing intensive care for severe burns.

Volcanoes can also cause various consequent hazards including tsunamis, break-out floods and lahars from volcanically dammed lakes, and ashfall. **An eruption may occur at any level of volcanic activity, and levels may not move in sequence as activity can change rapidly.** Some eruptions are explosive, blowing out great volumes of rock and molten material. Others erupt in flows, pouring out clouds of hot gas mixed with streams of liquid lava. People living in volcanic regions are at risk from ashfall, debris and lava flows.

The most widespread and disruptive hazard is usually volcanic ash. Ash can travel a long way depending on the wind, causing health problems for people and animals and damage to buildings and cars. Find out about the volcanic risk in your community. Talk to your Civil Defence Emergency Management Group to find out how they will warn you of a volcanic eruption.

Volcanic eruption hazards depend on the volcano and eruption style, and may include ash, ballistics (flying rocks), earthquakes, explosions, lahars, landslides, lava domes, lava flows, lightning, pyroclastic density currents (fast moving hot ash clouds), tsunamis and/or volcanic gases:

- Ash fall is the most likely volcanic hazard. **Volcanic ash** is comprised of small (less than 2mm), jagged pieces of rock and glass produced by explosive eruptions. Ash can be thick enough to collapse roofs even at a distance from the erupting volcano, especially if the ash is not removed from weaker structures and becomes wet and heavy. Volcanic ash can also disrupt air traffic, road transport and it can cause power and water outages. It's a good idea during an ashfall to disconnect downpipes so that ash on the roof of your house doesn't contaminate tank water or clog up public stormwater drains.

- **Earthquakes** can be caused by magma moving and pressure building inside or beneath a volcano.
- Changes to the ground surface, such as swelling, sinking or cracking, are often associated with volcanic unrest or as a result of volcanic eruption. **Land deformation** can directly damage homes, cause landslides and change the risk of flooding as the ground moves.
- **Lahars (volcanic mudflows)** are a hot or cold mixture of water and volcanic debris that flows rapidly downstream. Lahars form in a variety of ways, usually by the rapid melting of snow and ice by hot volcanic debris, intense rainfall on loose volcanic deposits, a breakout from a lake dammed by volcanic deposits or an eruption through a crater lake.
- **Lava flows** are streams of molten rock that pour from an eruption site and flow down valleys. You can generally avoid lava flows, as they usually cover new ground slowly, but they will destroy everything in their path.
- Volcanic unrest may be accompanied by increased **volcanic gas emissions**. Magma contains dissolved gases, which are released via the volcanic conduit into the atmosphere as magma approaches the Earth's surface. Carbon dioxide (CO_2) and sulphur gases such as hydrogen sulphide (H_2S) and sulphur dioxide (SO_2) are the hazardous gases that are most likely to be emitted during unrest.

If you are at risk of volcanic ash fall, add the following to your emergency supplies (the most at risk are residents of Tāmaki Makaurau Auckland, Te Moana-a-Toi Bay of Plenty, Tairāwhiti Gisborne, Te Matua-a-Māui Hawke's Bay, northern Manawatū, Te Tai Tokerau Northland, Taranaki and Waikato):

- Certified disposable dust masks (rated P2 or N95) and goggles.
- Plastic wrap or plastic sheeting (to keep ash out of electronics).
- Cleaning supplies including an air duster, a broom, a shovel and a vacuum cleaner with spare bags and filters.
- Heavy-duty plastic bags in which to dispose of ash.
- Sturdy footwear, gloves and clothing that covers your arms and legs.

WHAT TO DO DURING VOLCANIC ACTIVITY

- Follow official advice provided by your local Civil Defence Emergency Management Group, local authorities and emergency services, both during and following volcanic activity. For visitors to the Tongariro and Taranaki National Parks, follow advice from the Department of Conservation, which manages these sites.
- If you are in an exposed area and become aware of volcanic hazards the best way to protect yourself is to quickly move (run or drive if you can) as far as possible away from the volcano.
- If ash fall has been forecast for your region, before it starts, if possible, go home to avoid exposure to, and driving during, ash fall.
- Stay indoors. Volcanic ash is a health hazard, especially if you have respiratory difficulties such as asthma or bronchitis.

- If you have a visual impairment, wear eyeglasses. Do not wear contact lenses as trapped ash can scratch your eyes.
- Have a mask at hand – those used during Covid-19, while not perfect, will help.
- Close all windows and doors and shut down heat pumps to limit the entry of volcanic ash. Set up a single entry point for your house. Place damp towels at the threshold to prevent ash being tracked inside.
- Cover sensitive electronics. Do not remove covers until the indoor environment is completely ash free.
- Cover vehicles, machinery and spa pools to avoid any damage. Ash can corrode metal surfaces, cause abrasion damage to windscreens and paintwork, and clog air filters.
- Disconnect drainpipes/downspouts from gutters to stop the drains clogging. If you use a rainwater collection system for your water supply, disconnect the tank.
- Do not attempt to clear ash from your roof while ash is still falling.
- Keep your pets indoors.
- Keep gutters clear of leaves as hot ash could possibly ignite and set off a fire in the ceiling.

WHAT TO DO AFTER VOLCANIC ACTIVITY

Continue to follow official advice from your Civil Defence Emergency Management Group, local authorities and emergency services. If you have evacuated, do not return home until told it is safe to do so.

WILDFIRES

In a wildfire emergency, you may suddenly have to leave home for an extended period with little warning. The best thing you can do is prepare well and have your evacuation plan and grab bags ready. Roads could be closed, or traffic could build up; there's a chance you may be stranded in your car for some time. Keep a map of your evacuation routes with your evacuation plan.

When planning your escape route, you won't always know what direction the fire is coming from, so it's important to have more than one way out. Identify a safe zone in case you can't evacuate and you have to shelter in place (either on your property or within your community). A safe zone refers to a place that is clear of vegetation and can provide adequate refuge from an approaching fire, for example, large areas of concrete or short-grass school grounds, sports fields or a local beach.

WHAT TO DO DURING A WILDFIRE

If you have time before your evacuation, turn on any sprinklers you have around the house and wet materials like firewood that may fuel the fire. Some other considerations if time permits are:

- Move all vehicles to a safe location.
- Relocate lightweight garden furniture, door mats and other outdoor items indoors.
- Wet down the sides of buildings, decks and plants that are in the path of the wildfire.
- Close windows, doors and vents. Shut blinds, seal gaps under doors and windows with wet towels.
- Avoid breathing in wildfire smoke as the gases and particles can irritate the eyes, nose, throat and lungs, making it hard to breathe, causing coughing or wheezing, especially for those with asthma. A mask or cloth to cover your mouth may offer some assistance.
- Wildfires move quickly. If you can see the smoke or flames from a wildfire and you feel unsafe, don't wait for an official warning to leave. Call 111 if your life or property is threatened, or you can't evacuate on your own.

- The most dangerous places to find yourself are uphill or downwind from a fire. It's safest to stay upwind of fire. If the wind is blowing towards you and the fire, run into the wind. If the wind is blowing the fire in your direction, travel perpendicular to the fire to make your escape.
- If you're driving, stay in your car; it will offer some protection, at least from flames. Wind up the car's windows to keep out smoke and turn your lights on so you're visible to other motorists.

OTHER EMERGENCY SCENARIOS

Natural disasters aren't the only events we should be preparing for. We've seen in recent years the impact a pandemic can have on our society, as well as other 'man-made' disruptions such as infrastructure failure, cyber-attacks and terrorism, all of which are capable of causing massive dislocation, if not life-threatening consequences.

While terrorism and war, thankfully, don't occur as frequently in this part of the world as storms and earthquakes, it's important to keep continually appraised of national and international events in case there's the potential for 'cascade' events that might impact us here (for example, a war that could affect our imports of liquid fuel for transport).

PANDEMICS

One of the most threatening emergency situations is the outbreak of a new disease with high rates of illness and death. These outbreaks can quickly overwhelm local hospitals, healthcare providers and make it hard to maintain critical services.

An outbreak is characterised by the extent of the spread. It becomes a pandemic when the disease spreads throughout the world. Brand-new diseases can quickly become an epidemic or a pandemic if there is little or no immunity in the population. New Zealanders saw with Covid-19 in 2020–22 just how quickly a disease can spread and the effect it had on our lives.

CYBER-ATTACKS

Modern society is becoming increasingly dependent on computer systems and the internet, which are used to run the infrastructure that supports our dense, urban environments. As these systems grow more complex and more centralised, the cascade of potential repercussions on everyday life — the loss of electricity, the internet, the just-in-time logistics of distribution and so on — are a growing risk.

Computer systems can face disruptions due to human error (e.g., the worldwide computer outage of July 2024), intentional cyber-attacks, physical damage from secondary hazards and electro-magnetic pulses (EMP). Cyber-attacks are becoming more frequent and sophisticated and can take varying forms, including amateur hacking, 'hacktivism', ransomware attacks, cyber espionage or even sophisticated state-sponsored attacks. Attacks have the potential to cause internet or utility outages, leak or delete sensitive data and information, compromise critical infrastructure or services or cause physical destruction. More and more of our infrastructure and basic functions are connected to the internet: even traditionally non-computerised items (e.g., watches, thermostats, printers) are being connected to the internet, providing new avenues for hackers.

The biggest concern is an attack on critical infrastructure such as transportation, water or power systems. While manual backups still exist for these systems, overall service capabilities would be degraded if it were required that they revert to non-computerised technology.

If you have been affected by a cyber-attack, immediately disconnect all computers and devices from the network. When the all-clear has been given, reset and reinstall operating systems if necessary. If restoring from backups, ensure that these are free of malware.

INFRASTRUCTURE FAILURE

Infrastructure is the network of structures, utilities and facilities that supply and support our basic needs for mobility, power, water, sewerage and communications.

Infrastructure failures may arise from natural or technological hazards, human error, equipment failure or poor maintenance. Growing populations also put stress on infrastructure systems and assets that were built decades ago with lower-capacity designs. Updating or replacing these systems requires huge investments and can only happen slowly.

SPACE WEATHER

As if there weren't sufficient hazards to worry about here on Earth there are also extraterrestrial threats which, while remote (in more ways than one), can put a dent in things (ask the dinosaurs).

Space weather is most familiar to us Earthlings by way of the auroras – the Northern and Southern Lights

— that are the result of disturbances in the Earth's magnetosphere. These disturbances are caused by solar winds, created by ejections of material from the sun. Space weather can produce electromagnetic fields that can induce extreme currents in wires and disrupt power lines — even causing widespread power outages. They can also have disruptive and damaging impacts on computer systems, telephone systems and communications systems (including satellite networks and GPS services). Sudden bursts of plasma and magnetic-field structures from the sun's atmosphere — called coronal mass ejections — together with sudden bursts of radiation — solar flares — all cause effects here on Earth. The threat from solar flares is very real. The Carrington Event is famously the most intense geomagnetic storm in recorded history, peaking on 1–2 September 1859. It created strong auroral displays that were reported globally and caused sparking and even fires in multiple telegraph stations. A geomagnetic storm of this magnitude occurring today would cause widespread electrical disruptions, blackouts and damage due to extended outages of the electrical power grid.

PREPARING FOR A SPACE WEATHER EVENT

As for any other possible disruption, create a response plan that includes emergency communications, meeting places and the assembling of emergency supply kits for your home, car and work.

What to do during a space weather event

- Keep your electricity usage as low as possible.
- Follow advice of Civil Defence and emergency services.
- Disconnect electrical appliances if instructed to do so by local officials.

Landslides can happen without warning.

PREPARING AND SURVIVING

BEFORE YOU START

Emergencies and disasters often occur unexpectedly. Being prepared and having practised your responses beforehand will greatly increase your chances of coping and survival. It's not a bad idea to plan based on 'worst-case' and work backwards. Worst-case scenarios may not in fact eventuate but it's better to be safe than sorry. Plus, you'll have learnt a lot and gained a sense of achievement and satisfaction during the process.

KNOW, PREPARE, CONNECT

The underlying concept behind preparedness is to foster resilience to emergencies. Experience has shown that when people are aware of the hazards around them and plan their response accordingly, the impact of an emergency is significantly reduced. This allows people to cope better and recover more quickly.

During a major emergency, you, your household and your community could be isolated for days, maybe even weeks. Emergency services will be under heavy strain and unable to respond to everyone immediately. The most effective aid available to you will be those preparations you made beforehand.

Former generations knew about the importance of keeping enough stores of essentials in their homes as insurance against possible shortages. Not just 2–3 days' worth but enough to support households for 1–2 weeks should a disaster occur.

Surviving an emergency requires preparation, awareness and a calm approach. By staying informed, following your emergency plan and having essential supplies on hand, you can greatly increase your chances of staying safe. Remember, emergencies can happen at any time, so it's vital to be proactive and ready to protect yourself and your loved ones.

> **TRY TO STAY CALM IN ORDER TO STAY EFFECTIVE IN AN EMERGENCY.**

KEEP INFORMED

Vital to surviving any emergency is learning about the hazards that may strike your community, the risks you face from these hazards and your community's plans for warning and evacuation. Seek information from your local emergency management office or Red Cross. With weather events, keep up with forecasts and associated alerts. Be prepared to evacuate if necessary.

New Zealand's National Emergency Management Agency (NEMA) can contact the entire nation on very short notice with alerts sent to mobile phones. National radio and TV stations will also broadcast alerts. Learn what warnings and alerts are available from MetService and other government agencies as well.

EMERGENCY SUPPLY KITS AND GRAB BAGS

You may need to survive on your own for some time after an emergency. This means having your own food, water and other supplies in sufficient quantity to last for at least 3 days, although preferably for 2 weeks. Local officials and relief workers will be on the scene after an emergency, but they won't be able to reach everyone immediately. Basic services such as electricity, gas, water, sewage treatment and telephones may be cut off for days, or longer.

An emergency suppy kit is a collection of basic items that members of your household may need in the event of an emergency. Since you do not know where you will be when an emergency occurs, ideally prepare kits for home, work and your car, along with grab bags for each member of the household to take with them in case of an evacuation. Well-stocked emergency supply kits will make a significant contribution to your survival. Contents should include bottled water, non-perishable food, mobile phone (and charger), flashlight and batteries, a first aid kit, essential medications and a multi-tool.

EVACUATION

In most emergencies you should be able to stay in your home. If an official evacuation becomes necessary, follow the advice provided by local authorities. Additionally, there may be circumstances under which you and your household feel threatened or endangered and you need to leave your home, school or workplace to avoid these situations. The amount of time you have to leave will depend on the hazard. If the event is a weather condition, such as a storm that is being monitored, you might have a day or two to get ready. However, many emergencies allow no time for people to gather even the most basic necessities, which is why planning ahead is essential. Keep a full tank of gas in your car or your EV charged up if an evacuation seems likely. Gas stations may be unable to pump gas during power outages.

In an evacuation situation:

- Household members should have their grab bags ready.
- Wear sturdy shoes and clothing that provides warmth and weather protection.
- Listen to the news on a battery-powered radio, car radio or your mobile phone and follow local evacuation instructions.
- Secure your home — close and lock doors and windows.
- Unplug electrical equipment such as radios and televisions, and small appliances such as toasters and microwaves. Leave freezers and refrigerators plugged in unless there is a risk of flooding.
- Go immediately if you are instructed to evacuate. Let friends and family know where you are going.
- Do not drive into flooded areas.
- Stay away from downed power lines.

SAFETY SKILLS

It's important that household members know how to administer basic first aid, cardiopulmonary resuscitation (CPR) and how to use a fire extinguisher and where it is kept. Take a first aid and CPR class at your local branch of Red Cross or St John.

SHELTER

First think about the hazard and then choose a place in your home or another building that is safe against that hazard. For example, in the event of a tornado, you would decide on the basement or an interior room on the lowest level of your home away from corners, windows, doors and outside walls.

HELP OTHERS

It may be several days before emergency services can begin responding to individual communities and several months before normal infrastructure and utilities are back up and running. The most immediate source of help outside your own household will be your neighbours. Help each other where you can. Getting through a situation is easier and more effective as a group. Ensure your neighbours are aware of potential hazards. Help those who may need assistance and check in on the elderly especially and those with disabilities.

GIVE HELP, RECEIVE HELP.

CIVIL DEFENCE CENTRES AND COMMUNITY EMERGENCY HUBS

Civil Defence Centres (CDCs) or Emergency Assistance Centres (EACs) are a legislative requirement under the CDEM (Civil Defence Emergency Management) Act, so all regions in NZ have them, although they may not be in every town.

A Civil Defence Centre/Emergency Assistance Centre is a facility established and managed by councils during an emergency to assist those affected. They are open to the public and can be used for various purposes. A CDC/EAC would be opened when the community requires extensive assistance. The decision is based on each situation and the needs of the community.

'Evacuation centres' and 'welfare centres' are terms that can be used interchangeably but usually refer to CDCs/EACs.

Equally important is community preparedness. Communities are full of skilled and resourceful people, businesses, groups and facilities that can help solve many of the challenges that your community will face during and after an emergency. Official services are likely to be overwhelmed and not able to respond to every issue immediately. Instead, everyone will have to pitch in and help each other.

Community Emergency Hubs or 'Community Led Centres' are set-up and run by the community for the community. The Community Emergency Hub model was developed by the Wellington Region Emergency Management Office. The hubs act as a connection between those who need help and those who want to offer help in an emergency, a way for people to gather in their neighbourhood and work together to solve problems locally while still coordinating with councils about the big problems. Not all CDEM groups across New Zealand have these.

In a disaster, hubs act as places where neighbours can gather and share the skills and resources that already exist. They are not reliant on the physical building; they are merely a place from which to organise a community response. So, if the Hub becomes unsuitable, it can move to a better venue. Find out the location of Community Emergency Hubs near you.

INSURANCE

Check your insurance:

- Find out what your insurance policy covers, as well as what it doesn't cover.

- If you work through an insurance broker, ensure you know which insurer your policy is held with.
- Check that you will have enough insurance cover to rebuild your home and replace your contents after an emergency. Ideally, the cover includes the costs of emergency accommodation for a period.
- Review your insurance cover regularly to make sure it keeps pace with any change in the value of your home or contents, or any change in the costs to repair or rebuild your home.
- If you rent your home, it is strongly recommended that you have your own contents insurance. This will help to replace your belongings if they are lost or damaged. In addition, some contents insurance policies may include provision of temporary accommodation if the property you rent becomes uninhabitable.

Having insurance cover for your home and contents is important to help you get back on your feet after an emergency. Check your house insurance policy to see if it covers you for flood damage. Your private home insurance policy should include an amount for natural disaster insurance, which is provided by the Natural Hazards Commission (NHC). NHC provides insured homeowners with natural hazards cover to help rebuild or repair their homes and limited areas of land if they are damaged by a natural hazard event. You have natural hazards cover if you have a home insurance policy that includes fire insurance (and most do). The premium you pay your insurer includes a Natural Hazards Insurance levy (NHI levy), which gives you access to this natural hazards insurance. It's important to understand what is and isn't covered by NHI and by your insurer.

A QUICK GUIDE TO PREPAREDNESS AND ACTION

The preparedness and action essentials gathered here are common to or can be adapted for various emergency situations.

GETTING READY

Familiarising yourself with hazard threats and their potential for impact on your life, and then taking steps to deal with those impacts, is the very best thing you can do to protect yourself and your household. Being prepared for any emergency is as simple as planning ahead.

In an emergency event you should plan on the likelihood of having to look after yourself and your household for at least a week. Discuss with your household what this will mean and agree on a household emergency plan.

Begin planning by considering how you would cope if your daily life was suddenly and totally upended. Think about your daily activities, the people you care for or who rely on you, and how an emergency would change the way you live: if there was no power, no heating, no water, no phone or no internet. Sit down with members of your household and work out a plan that includes the basics of shelter, food and water, light and warmth, sanitation, communications and transport.

Include a contact sheet with all personal and work phone numbers so that everyone in the household knows how to contact each other. Also include a plan for emergency communications that includes establishing meeting places away from your home in case household members are separated.

EMERGENCY SUPPLY KITS AND GRAB BAGS

You may need to survive on your own for some time after an emergency. Local officials and relief workers will be on the scene, but they won't be able to reach everyone immediately. This means having your own food, water and other supplies — in sufficient quantity — to last for at least 3 days — ideally for 2 weeks, if you can. Basic services such as electricity, gas, water, sewage treatment and telephones may be cut off for days, or even longer.

An emergency supply kit is a collection of basic items that members of your household will need in the event of an emergency. Because you don't know where you will be when an emergency occurs, also prepare kits for your workplace and to carry in your car, along with grab bags for each member of your household to take with them if you have to evacuate suddenly.

Well-stocked emergency supply kits will help significantly in the event of an emergency. They should include bottled water, non-perishable food, mobile phone (and charger), flashlight and batteries, a first aid kit, essential medications and some kind of multi-tool.

EMERGENCY EVENTS

DURING AN EARTHQUAKE

While an earthquake is happening, your best defence is to **DROP**, **COVER** and **HOLD**.

- **DROP** down onto your hands and knees.
- **COVER** your head and neck (or your entire body if possible) under a sturdy table or desk (if it is within a few steps of you). If there is no shelter nearby, cover your head and neck with your arms and hands.
- **HOLD** on to your shelter (or your position to protect your head and neck) until the shaking stops. If the shaking shifts your shelter around, move with it.

DURING FLOODING

Be prepared to evacuate and keep your grab bag nearby. Listen to emergency services and local Civil Defence authorities. Follow any instructions about evacuations of your area. Self-evacuate if you feel unsafe. **Don't take any chances, and act quickly if you see rising water.**

- If your home is at risk of flooding, move household items out of the reach of flood-waters. Have tarpaulins on hand to help keep your belongings dry. Think about having sandbags ready to use.
- Move valuable and dangerous items as high above the floor as possible. This includes electrical equipment and chemicals. Use watertight containers to store important items.
- Floods and flash floods can happen quickly. If you see rising water do not wait for official warnings. Head for higher ground and stay away from flood-water.
- Never try to walk, swim or drive through flood-water. Many flood deaths are vehicle-related — caused by driving through flood-water or attempting to move a

stranded vehicle. Attempting to walk through floodwater — unless absolutely necessary — is also not recommended. Children, especially, may be at risk of being swept away.

- Stay up to date with the latest weather information from MetService. Pay attention to weather Watches and Warnings.

DURING A LANDSLIDE

Evacuate immediately if it is safe to do so. Seek higher ground outside the path of the landslide. The side of your house furthest from the landslide is likely to be the safest location within your property.

DURING A STORM

- Identify a safe location in your home to gather during a major storm. This should ideally be away from windows, skylights or glass doors, as these can be broken by strong winds or hail and cause damage or injury.
- Close all windows, curtains and blinds to prevent possible injury from flying glass.
- If a power line falls onto a car, it may still be live and liven the car. Do not try to rescue people from cars trapped by fallen lines, wait for professional help. If you are the one inside a car trapped by a fallen line, stay there and phone for help and wait until the line has been made safe.

DURING A TSUNAMI

If you are near the coast when an earthquake strikes, **DROP, COVER** and **HOLD**, and if the earthquake is **LONG OR STRONG, GET GONE**. As soon as the shaking stops, move immediately to the nearest high ground or as far inland as you can get. Every metre makes a difference. Don't wait for an official tsunami warning.

Aftershocks may generate another tsunami. Stay away from coastal water, tidal estuaries, rivers and streams for at least 24 hours after any tsunami or tsunami warning.

DURING VOLCANIC ACTIVITY

If you are in an exposed area and become aware of volcanic activity, the best way to protect yourself is to quickly move (run or drive if you can) as far away as possible from the volcano. If ashfall has been forecast for your region, avoid driving if possible and stay inside.

DURING A WILDFIRE

If you have time before evacuating, move your vehicles to a safe location, wet down decks and the sides of buildings, and close all windows, doors, vents and blinds. Seal gaps under doors and windows with wet towels.

Try to get to safe zones; areas that are clear of vegetation and which may provide adequate refuge from an approaching fire such as large areas of concrete or short-grass school grounds, sports fields or local beaches.

Wildfires move quickly. If you can see the smoke or flames from a wildfire and you feel unsafe, don't wait for an official warning to leave. Call 111 if your life or property is threatened, or you can't evacuate on your own.

SHELTER

Firstly, think about the hazard and then choose a place in your home or at another location where you and your family will be safe. If your situation is dire don't wait for any official notice of evacuation — **just GO!**

If you find yourself in need of temporary shelter, tents are an option, as is your car. If you don't have a tent, then you can easily set up an emergency shelter using a tarpaulin and some rope or cord. Tie the rope or chord between 2 poles or trees and lay the tarpaulin over it. Your car can also offer protection from the elements. Keep your car fuelled or charged.

INSURANCE

For homeowners: Check your insurance to confirm exactly what your policy covers, as well as what it doesn't. Check that you will have enough insurance cover to rebuild your home and replace your contents after an emergency. Ideally the insurance cover should include the costs of emergency accommodation for a period.

For renters: It's strongly recommended that you have contents insurance. Some contents insurance policies may include provision of temporary accommodation if the property you rent becomes uninhabitable.

Make a record of your personal property, in as much detail as possible, for insurance purposes. Take photos or a video of the interior and exterior of your home as a record.

UTILITY SHUT-OFF AND SAFETY

In the event of an emergency, you may need to shut off one or more of the utility services — water, gas or electricity — that connect to your home. Take care when checking the connections. Keep people away from fallen power lines.

WATER SHUT-OFF

Water quickly becomes a precious resource during many emergencies. It is vital that all household members learn how to shut off the water at the main valve as cracked or broken water lines can pollute the water supply to your house. Shut off your water until you hear from authorities that it is safe for drinking.

In an emergency, water can be obtained from a number of places within your home, such as the hot water cylinder and toilet cisterns.

GAS SHUT-OFF

If you think you smell gas, it's important that you leave the immediate area and contact your gas supplier as there may be a leak. This is because gas is highly flammable, which means if there's a leak, combined with the likes of a spark from lighting a candle, flicking a light switch or using a mobile phone, it could ignite and lead to an explosion or fire.

If you smell gas inside your house:

- Open a window.
- Turn off gas appliances.
- Don't smoke (including e-cigarettes) and extinguish any naked flames.
- Don't use any electrical equipment, switches, mobile phones or electronic equipment.
- Vacate the building.

Avoid turning off piped gas supplies unless absolutely necessary as any closed-off supply to a house requires a professional to reconnect it.

ELECTRICITY SHUT-OFF

Make sure everyone in the household knows how to turn off the electricity at the main switchboard inside your home if there is an emergency. It's recommended that you first turn off individual appliances including fridge and freezer (keep fridge and freezer doors closed – most freezers will keep food at a safe temperature for up to 24 hours as long as the doors stay closed) before switching the main switch to the OFF position.

Turn electronics – TVs, computers, stereos – off at the wall.

Power can surge when restored, possibly damaging sensitive electronics. It's a good idea to check that stove elements and heaters are also turned off; this will ensure they don't come back on without you noticing when the electricity has been restored. Leave on an overhead light so you can see when the power is back on.

EMERGENCY TOILETS

No running water means no flushing toilets. The wastewater network (which takes away the water we pour down the sink and our toilet waste) is even more vulnerable than the drinking water network – its broken pipes will take longer to find and fix and there are more of them. You may not be able to use your normal toilet for some time after a major earthquake or other emergency so you will need to think about what you can use for an emergency toilet, such as the two-bucket system or a long drop.

IMPORTANT DOCUMENTS

Keep up to date with essential documentation as it relates to the household and to household members. Store important documents such as insurance policies, property records and other important papers in a safe place such as a safety deposit box away from your home. For a backup and to ensure against the loss of paper documents in the event of emergency, photograph them with your mobile phone or scan them to create a digital inventory that can be saved to a memory stick. Print out copies of important documents to keep with you in your grab bags.

Make copies of documents such as your driver's licence, bank account numbers, insurance policy numbers, business documents and your emergency contact list. Save these to your mobile phone.

EMERGENCY FIRST AID

For immediate emergency first aid assistance call 111 — in the meantime:

- **Bleeding** — Apply pressure to wounds to staunch the bleeding. Raise limb injuries to above the level of the heart to slow bleeding. If the wound continues to bleed, continue to apply fresh compresses, one on top of another. Do not use a tourniquet unless you are a professional.
- **Burns** — Cover burns with sterile bandages, or a clean loose cloth, kept loose over the wound.
- **Broken bones** — If it appears the person has neck or spine injuries, don't move them unless absolutely necessary. With other breaks, stop any bleeding and immobilise the limb or joint.

- **Hypothermia** – Remove the person's wet clothes, get them into dry clothing, ensuring you cover their head, hands and feet. Wrap them in a dry sleeping bag or use the body heat of another person. Give warm drinks.
- **Cardiac arrest** – If the person is not breathing normally, start cardiopulmonary resuscitation (CPR), a combination of chest compressions and rescue breathing that provides oxygen to the lungs and keeps oxygenated blood circulating until an effective heartbeat and regular breathing can be restored. **Chest compressions are the most important part of CPR** – even if you can't or don't wish to provide rescue breathing.

EMERGENCY COMMUNICATIONS

There are multiple ways to stay informed during an emergency including radio, news media, your local emergency management office and local council channels, TV and Emergency Mobile Alerts. Knowing the natural warning signs for a tsunami is important too.

Emergency Mobile Alerts are alerts that can be sent to your mobile phone, without needing to sign up or download an app. Most mobile phones are capable of receiving these alerts.

Authorities will only send Emergency Mobile Alerts when there is a threat to life or significant disruption.

- Use your mobile phone to share your location with members of your household and vice versa. Know how to find your GPS position on your mobile phone so you can advise someone looking for you.
- Text rather than call during an emergency to preserve bandwidth for emergency services and not clog up phone lines.

- Have a plan with your household for how you can reconnect with each other in an emergency event.
- Agree where you would go if you can't go home or get to your meeting place.
- If you work or go to school in different places, consider how you will reconnect with each other.
- Identify friends or family that you could stay with if you can't go home.
- Make a note of the frequency for your local radio stations in your emergency plan.

USEFUL TIPS

- Always keep your car's gas tank at least half full and your EV charged up. Gas stations rely on electricity to power their pumps, and an EV won't get very far if it can't be charged.
- Know where the manual release lever of your electric garage door opener is and how to operate it. Otherwise, if the power is out and your car is stuck in the garage, you're stuck, too.
- Have extra batteries for powering lights and radios, and power packs or small solar panels for charging your phone, laptop and other devices. Remember that you can also charge-up using the USB slots in your car, so it's smart to keep a phone charging cable in your car.
- Stay informed. Listen to a battery-powered radio or car radio to keep up with news and weather. Follow the instructions of Civil Defence and emergency services.
- Keep a torch, battery-powered lantern, and spare batteries handy. A rechargeable torch is a good investment.
- If you're notified of a planned water outage, keep buckets of water nearby on the day for flushing the toilet. Fill up the bath as well.

- Pack a manually operated can opener with your emergency food supplies.
- When dealing with flooded roads, the advice when it comes to safety is simply don't drive your vehicle through flood-waters.
- Check on your neighbours and anyone who may need your help ahead of an emergency.
- Keep some cash at home in a safe place. In a major emergency in which the electricity supply is lost it won't be possible to get cash from ATMs nor to make payments electronically. Have the cash in small denomination notes to simplify purchases.

MAKING PLANS

Being prepared for any emergency is as simple as planning ahead. A household emergency plan will not only provide a structure for you to follow and allow you to respond quickly and safely when an event happens, but also reduces anxiety around potential emergencies. At the same time, bear in mind that situations can escalate suddenly. Be flexible and be ready to change your plan if you have to.

Essential to the household emergency plan is knowing information such as:

- Where the emergency food and water survival kits are kept.
- The safest way out of the house.
- The whereabouts of gas, water and electricity mains and how to turn them off.
- Where to shelter in the event of various emergencies.
- Who is responsible for checking essential items regularly.
- How to contact household members during an emergency (if you are not all together).
- Who is responsible for the safety of any pets.

THINK OF YOUR NEEDS AND THE CORRESPONDING ACTIONS.

HOUSEHOLD EMERGENCY PLAN

Sit down with members of your household and work out a plan that includes the basics of shelter, food and water, light and warmth, sanitation, communications and transport. Include a contact sheet with all personal and work phone numbers so that everyone in the household knows how to contact each other if they get separated. Think about your daily activities, the people you care for or who rely on you and how an emergency would change the way you live.

- **Stuck at home** – Being at home may mean being without power and water or any way to get supplies for a week or more. Do you have enough food and water? What about those who need medication, do you have enough stored? Do you have enough food and water for your pets, too?
- **Can't get home** – In an emergency, public transport may not be running, and roads and neighbourhoods may be blocked off. Talk to your household about how you will get in touch and where you will meet in an emergency. If you can't take your normal route home, how will you get there? Where will you meet other members of your household if your street is a no-go zone? Make sure you know your school or early childhood centre's emergency plans.
- **Have to evacuate** – Some houses, streets and neighbourhoods may not be safe to stay in and you may have to leave in a hurry. If your street is evacuated, where will you go? What will you take? What about pets? Do your neighbours need your help?
- **Check your zone** – If you live in a tsunami evacuation zone, make sure your evacuation place is outside of the zone.

- **No power** – What would you do if the power was out for days? What if there were no lights at night? And what about cooking and keeping warm? Power cuts could affect EFTPOS and ATM machines, in which case, make sure you have some cash at home to pay for groceries at the local supermarket; otherwise have sufficient supplies to see you through a week or more. Make sure everyone knows where the torches and batteries are. Have a solar or battery-powered radio so you can keep up with the latest news and alerts. Know which radio stations to tune in to for information during an emergency.
- **No water** – Water supplies could be affected in an emergency. How would you wash, cook, clean? What would you drink? Store drinking water, and think about emergency sources of water.
- **Stock up on food** – Put together a special store of food for emergencies, that doesn't need to be cooked (e.g., canned food) and have a gas barbecue or camping stove to cook on.
- **No phone or internet** – What will you do if the phone and internet goes down? How will you keep in touch, arrange meet up points and keep up with news and weather alerts? In an emergency, phone lines can become overloaded quickly. Help keep them clear so emergency calls can get through. Use text or online messaging to keep in touch if communication isn't urgent. Everyone in the household should have a written list of important phone numbers in addition to the contacts list on their mobile phones.

Your household emergency plan should also include an evacuation plan and meet-up locations. You may not be together when emergency strikes, so it's important to know how you'll reconnect if separated. Panic and chaos are quick to erupt during a crisis; having a plan helps reduce the risk of forgetting things.

Set meeting-up points for you and your household that are based on proximity to the locations you spend the most time. For example, your child's school, your home and your place of work should all be options when determining meet-up locations. Depending on the emergency you're dealing with, your meet-up location may be destroyed or become inaccessible, or road closures may prevent you from returning to your house, and communication by mobile phone may not be possible. Have a backup site, some centrally located place to which everyone can walk, such as a nearby park.

Draw up a map of your evacuation routes and keep a copy of it with your evacuation plan and ensure each member of the household has a copy. The evacuation plan should include information on:

- Escape routes.
- Household communications.
- Utility shut-off and safety.
- Insurance and vital records.
- Special needs.
- Caring for pets.

Practise your plan to check that it works for all members of your household and fine-tune as necessary. Regular practice is also practice in remaining calm and being able to respond quickly when an emergency does occur, in the way of the military concept of 'What is difficult in training will become easy in a battle' – in short, 'Train hard, fight easy'.

Knowing *instinctively* what to do could mean the difference between life and death. Review the plan frequently; things change.

ESCAPE ROUTES

Draw a floorplan of your home, using a blank sheet of paper for each floor. Mark 2 escape routes from each room. Pin a copy of the drawings at eye level in each child's room and on the fridge and make sure children understand the drawings. Establish places to meet in the event of an emergency, for example, the next-door neighbour's telephone pole or if a meet-up location near your house is a problem, then arrange somewhere outside the immediate area, at, say, the local park.

Some emergencies may require evacuation from your home. Familiarise yourself with evacuation routes in your area and look for multiple ways to leave your neighbourhood. Practise driving these routes – at night as well as during the daytime – so you're confident using them in an emergency. Have a set of paper maps in case GPS is not available. If evacuation is not possible, sort out a safe room within your home where you can take shelter.

HOUSEHOLD COMMUNICATIONS

Your household may not be together when an emergency strikes, so plan how you will contact one another in different situations. Make up a contact card for each household member and have them keep these cards handy in a wallet, purse or backpack. Create a backup by emailing the file to yourself and including a copy in your household emergency supply kit.

A household communications plan should also outline how you will communicate after an emergency. Text messages may get through in overloaded telecommunications infrastructure, whereas phone calls may not. Social media can also help you stay connected and create back-up pathways for communication.

UTILITY SHUT-OFF AND SAFETY

In the event of an emergency, you may need to shut off one or more of the utility services — water, gas or electricity — to your home.

- **Water** quickly becomes a precious resource during many emergencies. It is vital that all household members know where the main house valve is and how to turn it off as cracked or broken water lines can pollute the water supply to your house. Make sure that it is completely shut off: your valve may be stuck in the open position, or it may only partially close. Don't turn your water back on until you hear from authorities that it is safe for drinking.
- **Gas** leaks and explosions are responsible for a significant number of fires following emergencies. It is vital that all household members know how to shut off the mains gas. Contact your local gas company for guidance on preparation and response regarding gas appliances and gas service to your home and learn the proper shut-off procedure. (Be sure not to actually turn off the gas when practising as reconnection requires a professional.) In an emergency situation, if you smell gas or hear a blowing or hissing noise, open a window and get everyone out quickly. Turn off the gas if you can and call the gas company.

- **Electricity** sparks have the potential to ignite natural gas if there is a leak. Make sure everyone in your household knows where the main switchboard is and how to turn off the electricity.

INSURANCE, IMPORTANT DOCUMENTS AND MONEY

Keep up with essential documentation as it relates to your household and to your household members. Store important documents such as insurance policies, property records and other papers in a safe place, such as a safety deposit box away from your home. For a backup, and to ensure against the loss of paper documents, photograph them with your mobile phone or scan them to create a digital inventory that can be saved to a memory stick. Print out copies of important documents to go into your emergency grab bag.

Review your existing insurance policies and make sure they provide coverage for property, contents and vehicles. Check you have in place what is required for you and your household to be fully covered in the event of an emergency. Revise your coverage if not.

Make a record of your personal property, in as much detail as possible, for insurance purposes. Take photos or a video of the interior and exterior of your home as well as of your personal belongings.

Keep some cash at home in a safe place. In a major emergency in which the electricity supply is lost, it won't be possible to get cash from ATMs or to make payments electronically. Have the cash in small denomination notes to simplify purchases.

SPECIAL NEEDS

If you or someone close to you has a disability or a special need, you may have to take additional steps with your preparation and action during an emergency. Hearing-impaired people may need to make special arrangements to receive warnings while mobility-impaired may need special assistance to evacuate. Look into getting an uninterruptible power supply (UPS) for someone in your household relying on an electrically powered machine to assist their health, such as a chronic obstructive pulmonary disease (COPD) patient.

PETS

Pets will also be affected by emergencies. Ahead of such events, gather pet supplies and ensure your pet has proper ID and up-to-date veterinarian records. Have a pet carrier for smaller animals and a leash for larger animals. Review your pet insurance policy if you have it. Make sure that kennels or cages are set on higher ground to avoid getting caught in possible flooding.

Go through the different plans for different emergencies with your household on a regular basis; familiarise yourselves and practise, so that what needs to be decided and what needs to happen will come naturally and quickly to mind if the occasion ever arises. Adapt your plan and response as the situation unfolds. Familiarise yourself with where local assembly/ evacuation areas and Community Emergency Hubs are. Discuss with your children what a disruption or emergency may mean for them, from loss of electricity through to evacuation. It's a good idea to put up copies of all the various plans — the household emergency plan, escape routes — somewhere you can continually refer to them.

By looking after yourself and your household, you'll also be helping emergency services focus their limited resources on the people who need the most help.

MAKE SURE EVERYONE IN YOUR HOUSEHOLD KNOWS WHAT TO DO.

GRAB BAG CHECKLIST

Remember: Don't include so many items that your bag becomes too heavy to carry!

- [ ] Comfortable backpack
- [ ] Water and snacks
- [ ] Walking shoes
- [ ] First aid kit
- [ ] Emergency blanket
- [ ] Torch
- [ ] Radio (battery/wind up)
- [ ] Hand sanitiser
- [ ] Rain jacket or poncho
- [ ] Warm jacket
- [ ] Cash
- [ ] Medication & Prescriptions
- [ ] Portable phone charger
- [ ] Toiletries
- [ ] Baby supplies
- [ ] Pet supplies
- [ ] Notebook & pen
- [ ] Copies of important documents
- [ ] Face covering/mask
- [ ] Spare underwear
- [ ] Hat/sun protection
- [ ] Other items you rely on

Find out more at **wremo.nz/grab-bags**

WELLINGTON REGION EMERGENCY MANAGEMENT OFFICE

PROMPTS

- Try to remain calm when putting your emergency plan into action.
- Email your household emergency plan and evacuation plan to all members of the household.
- Keep plans and copies of important documents on a USB stick and keep this in your grab bag.
- Work out ahead of time what each person in your household will do in the event of an emergency.
- Know where emergency items are stored and who is to be responsible for maintaining supplies.
- If someone in your household relies on special equipment or medications make sure your planning includes how to make sure those special needs will be dealt with.
- Decide what each person in the household will have in their grab bag and where you will keep the grab bags.
- Have a plan for looking after your pets.
- Know how and when to turn off the water and electricity in your home or business. Turn off gas only if you suspect a leak, or if you are instructed to do so by authorities.
- Make a note of which radio stations to listen to and which social media accounts to connect with for Civil Defence information during an emergency event.
- Contact your nearest Civil Defence Emergency Management Group for assistance in an emergency.
- **Phone 111 if lives or property are at risk.**

EMERGENCY SUPPLY KITS AND GRAB BAGS

***Store this book in your Emergency Supply Kit. If the power goes out, you may not be able to access the internet.**

Some emergencies may require you to stay at home and others may mean you need to evacuate your home. While some emergency events may be resolved in just a few days – such as an electricity outage – others could impact normal daily life for considerably longer. Having enough supplies for everyone in your household – food and water – for at least 3 days should be your aim, but ideally you should gather enough for 1–2 weeks. For some people, the financial outlay to cover a long period may be a hindrance. Do what you can – anything is better than nothing at all.

Ideally, you will be self-sufficient for 7 days. However, don't forget neighbours can help each other out by sharing resources, such as gas for a camping stove. (Keep in mind that you will already have many of the items you will want for getting through an emergency in your home, such as blankets and sleeping bags, camping stoves and barbecues, torches, etc.)

By looking after yourself and your household, you'll also be helping emergency services focus their limited resources on the people who are most in need of help.

Putting together a basic emergency supply kit for your household will help you get through until the emergency event is over and usual resources are available again. The time and expense involved in making up a comprehensive store of items can be done gradually, purchasing 1 or 2 items during each weekly shop. Some items, such as spare sets of warm clothes, you'll probably already have on hand.

In addition to having emergency supplies stocked up for staying in your home, you should also assemble smaller emergency supply kits for your workplace and car, as well as individual grab bags of supplies.

HOUSEHOLD EMERGENCY SUPPLY KIT

This is the basic household kit and comprises essential food, water and supplies for at least 3 days, or for much longer if possible. Keep the kit in a designated place and have it ready in case you have to leave your home quickly. Make sure all household members know where the kit is kept. Place items in airtight plastic bags and store everything in one or more easily carried containers, such as a lidded plastic carry box, duffle bag or cardboard cartons.

Recommended items:

- 3-day supply of non-perishable food and 3-day supply of water — 3 litres of water per person per day (3 litres is what you'll need for drinking and basic hygiene but more will be required for things like cleaning dishes).

- If you are able to, increase supply of food and water to 1 week's, or even 2 weeks' worth (the more self-sufficient you can be in the face of a major emergency, the better).
- A large plastic bucket with a tight lid (or large rubbish bags), toilet paper and disinfectant, to be used as an emergency toilet.
- A small fire extinguisher.
- A solar- or battery-powered radio (or your car radio will also work) so you can keep up with the latest news and alerts.
- Barbecue or camping stove and a lighter (matches, gas-filled cigarette lighter or other fire-lighting device, firelighter tablets to start fire). Make sure you have enough fuel to last at least 3 days.
- Boots (work and/or gumboots).
- Cash in small denominations (ATMs, EFTPOS machines and online bank transfers may not work during an emergency event).
- Copies of your important documents (see pg 90).
- Duct tape.
- Dust masks (rated P2 or N95) and work gloves to protect yourself. Masks can be useful in emergencies caused by several different hazards: pandemics, volcanic eruptions or when cleaning up after a flood or tsunami.
- Emergency plan.
- Extra clothing. You should at least have 1 complete change of clothing and shoes per person, including a jacket or coat, long pants, long-sleeve shirt, hat, mittens, and scarf.
- First aid kit (fully stocked) and instruction manual.
- Flashlight and extra batteries.
- Hand soap and/or disinfecting hand cleaner gel that does not require water.

- Items for infants, such as formula, nappies and bottles.
- Kitchen accessories and cooking utensils, including a mechanical can opener, paper plates, cups, plastic utensils, cooking foil and paper towels.
- Large plastic trash bags (for use with trash, waste, water protection, ground cloth or as a temporary blanket).
- Mobile phone and charger.
- Other items to meet your unique household needs: If you live in a cold climate, you must think about warmth. It is possible that you will not have heat. Think about your clothing and bedding supplies.
- Pack of cards (optional).
- Paper maps.
- Pen and paper.
- Photocopies of credit cards and identification cards.
- Plastic seal-lock bags.
- Rapid setting glue.

Start with a home emergency supply kit/store of food and water, then grab bags for each person in your household. If you can, also an emergency supply kit for your car and your workplace. It sounds like a lot, but you don't know where you'll be when an emergency happens nor how quickly you may have to evacuate.

- Rubber gloves.
- Sanitation and hygiene items.
- Sleeping bags/duvets/blankets.
- Spare set of keys to your house and vehicles.
- Special needs items, such as prescription medications, glasses, contact lens solutions and hearing-aid batteries.
- Tarpaulins and rope/cord.
- USB chargers and/or portable charging devices (such as power banks) to charge your mobile phone. Some solar- and battery-powered radios can also be used to charge phones.
- Water purification system – chlorine to amount specified.
- Whistle.

CAR EMERGENCY SUPPLY KIT

This is a smaller, more portable kit with a lot of the same content you'll have in your household kit. You'll want enough supplies to tide you over for several days.

Plan for what you will do if you're in your car when an emergency happens. You may have had to evacuate your home, or you may be stranded in your vehicle. A major traffic accident, flood or snowstorm can make it impossible to get home. In the event that your car is suddenly your temporary home, having a well-outfitted car emergency supply kit will allow you and others to have a comfortable and safe place if you can't get home or find a motel room.

In addition to the basic food and water supplies, you should have vehicle safety items – for example, a properly inflated spare tyre, wheel wrench and jack, hazard flares, jumper cables – plus a grab bag and a first aid kit with you. Also, keep a spare pair of walking shoes, a pair of gumboots, a waterproof jacket, essential medicines, snack food, water, a phone charger and a torch in your car.

Additional items you could also include in your car emergency supply kit: a fire extinguisher, bottled water, non-perishable food, medications, toilet paper and hand sanitiser.

- If driving in extreme winter conditions or cold climates, you should add a windshield scraper, brush, shovel, tyre chains and warm clothing. Blankets or sleeping bags will help keep you warm in case of an emergency.
- A portable gas stove, shovel, tarpaulin, large clean-sacks and a tent.

It's a good idea to always keep a decent amount of fuel in your car's tank in case of an emergency. Petrol stations may not be able to operate pumps if there are power cuts, or roads may be blocked or damaged, preventing you from getting to a petrol station.

GRAB BAG

A grab bag is a small bag or backpack of essential items that you can carry with you if you have to evacuate your home or workplace with little warning. Have grab bags made up for everyone in your household.

You may need to evacuate on foot, so distribute items among the members of your household, ensuring what you are taking is not too heavy or bulky. Consider having emergency survival items and a grab bag stored in your car and at work.

Everyone — including children — should have their own bag with their own supply of water and snack foods, warm clothes and copies of their important documents and photo ID. Keep grab bags where you can access them in a hurry.

Basic supplies to have in a grab bag in case you must evacuate:

- Cash — in small denomination notes plus some coins as well.
- A change of clothes (wind/waterproof/winter clothing and strong outdoor shoes).
- Chargers for your phone and any other devices you may need.
- Copies of your important documents and photo ID.
- A copy of your household's emergency and contact plans.
- Emergency water and easy-to-carry food rations such as energy bars and dried foods.

Optional extras for some grab bags include:

- First aid kit and prescription medicine.
- Hand sanitiser.
- House keys, car keys, work keys (get a few spare sets of all of these made up).
- Space blankets — these can save a life when faced with cold and wet weather. A regular sleeping bag or blanket will also work.
- A pocket knife or multi-tool.
- Radio (solar, wind up or battery powered — with spare batteries).
- Small plastic bags.
- A small towel.
- Spare set of eyeglasses and/or contact lenses.
- Toiletries — towel, soap, toothbrush, sanitary items, toilet paper.

- Torches and spare batteries — a headlamp torch will allow you to be handsfree.

WHAT YOU SHOULD PACK IN YOUR WORKPLACE EMERGENCY SUPPLY KIT

A workplace kit should fit in one container or bag, ready to 'grab and go' in case you have to evacuate from your workplace. Make sure you have food and water in the kit. Its contents should match what you pack in your grab bag.

MAINTAINING YOUR EMERGENCY SUPPLY KITS

Check your emergency supply kits and update their contents once a year.

- Store food in closed containers such as lidded plastic bins. On the top or side of the containers write the date you stored the food .
- Use foods before their expiry and replace with fresh supplies.
- Place new items at the back of the storage area and older ones in the front.

PROMPTS

- Check all batteries every 3 months. Battery-powered lighting is the safest and easiest. Do not use candles as they can tip over during aftershocks or in a gust of wind. Do not use kerosene lamps, they require a great deal of ventilation and are not designed for indoor use.
- You don't have to have all your emergency supplies in one place, but you might have to find them in a hurry and/or in the dark. Make sure everyone in your household knows where everything is.

Continued over page

- Aim for a minimum of 3 days' food and water – you can build up to this over time by storing an extra tin of food here and there, gradually increasing the amount of basic food you keep at home. If you can, stock up for a longer duration in case of a pandemic or major hazard event, but keep in mind that even a few items are better than none in ensuring you are able to cope if an emergency event happens.
- Check expiry dates every 6 months and follow the practice of 'first-in, first-out'.
- Ask your GP for an extra week's supply of any prescription medicines to keep in your emergency supply kit.
- Store water in clean plastic containers.
- Neighbours can help each other out by sharing resources like barbecues and portable gas stoves.
- Make sure you're able to find your supplies in the dark and that everyone in your household knows where the torches and spare batteries are.
- It doesn't matter how you store your emergency supplies, just as long as you have everything on hand.
- Keep emergency supplies and your mobile phone in places where they're not likely to be knocked over or buried by falling objects – under a strong table, for example.

FIRST AID ESSENTIALS

Knowing even a few of the basics of first aid could be of critical importance during an emergency (not to mention in everyday life). Contact your local Red Cross or St John for first aid information and courses. In preparing to deal with hazard emergencies, you should keep first aid kits in your home, workplace, car and grab bags.

Remember to include any prescription drugs you need with your emergency survival items. Because the storage requirements of prescription drugs vary, some may have to be added to your first aid kit at the last minute, such as those stored in the fridge. Tape a note to the outside of your first aid kit container reminding you to take along prescription drugs if you have to evacuate.

A FIRST AID KIT

Commercially available first aid kits — you can also purchase these from St John or the Red Cross — are a good basis for a kit that you can gradually expand to provide a more comprehensive kit suited to most, if not all, emergencies.

Suggested contents for a basic first aid kit:

- Plasters (in a variety of sizes and shapes).
- Sterile gauze dressings (small, medium and large).
- Sterile eye dressings (at least 2).
- Triangular bandages.
- Crêpe rolled bandages.
- Scissors.
- Safety pins.
- Disposable sterile gloves.
- Cleansing wipes.
- Sticky tape.
- Cream or spray to relieve insect bites and stings.
- Antiseptic cream.
- Hand sanitiser.

- Painkillers, such as paracetamol (and infant paracetamol for children).
- Cough medicine.
- Antihistamine cream or tablets.
- Eye wash and eye bath.

Keep a basic first aid manual with your first aid kit. Red Cross also offers a first aid app that provides a free and comprehensive guide to first aid and emergency response.

EMERGENCY FIRST AID

For immediate emergency first aid assistance call 111 – in the meantime:

- **Bleeding** – Apply pressure to the wound to staunch bleeding. Raise limb injuries to above the level of the heart to help slow bleeding. If the wound continues to bleed, keep applying fresh compresses, one on top of another. Do not use a tourniquet unless you are a professional.
- **Burns** – Cover burns with sterile bandages or a clean loose cloth kept loose over the wound.
- **Broken bones** – If it appears the person has neck or spine injuries, don't move them unless absolutely necessary. With other breaks, stop any bleeding and immobilise the limb or joint.
- **Hypothermia** – Remove the person's wet clothes, get them into dry clothing, ensuring you cover their head, hands and feet. Wrap them in a dry sleeping bag or use the body heat of another person. Give warm drinks.
- **Cardiac arrest** – If the person is not breathing normally, start cardiopulmonary resuscitation (CPR), a combination of chest compressions and rescue breathing that provides oxygen to the lungs and

keeps oxygenated blood circulating until an effective heartbeat and regular breathing can be restored. Chest compressions are the most important part of CPR — even if you can't or don't wish to provide rescue breathing. Contact your local St John or Red Cross branch for information on CPR and first aid courses.

PROMPTS

- Take a first aid course.
- Depending on circumstances, it's possible emergency services may not be able to get to people in the first day(s) of an emergency. In the meantime, do what you can to provide first aid to any injured or ill.
- Get to know your neighbours, and then when something happens, you'll be able to help each other while emergency services and Civil Defence are busy helping people who need them the most.

CHEST COMPRESSIONS ARE THE MOST IMPORTANT PART OF CPR. IF YOU CAN'T GIVE RESCUE BREATHING TO THE PERSON, CONTINUE WITH CHEST COMPRESSIONS, PUSHING HARD AND FAST.

SHELTER

While some emergency events — such as an electricity outage — may mean being stuck at home for a few days, others — such as flooding — may necessitate your needing to evacuate. Be prepared for both eventualities.

SHELTER

Make your home your meeting place but have an alternative just in case you can't get there. If you do decide to stay in-place, keep to the rooms where you'll be the safest. In a storm event, for instance, choose a room with the least number of windows as these can break during strong winds. If there are windows, tape or cover them with wood or plastic sheeting to reduce the danger to you and your household.

STAYING IN PLACE

Your home remains the best place to shelter during an emergency, if it is safe. Things to keep in mind when sheltering at home:

- Make sure your water supply is always completely safe.
- Make a checklist for everything you need to stock in your home and prepare for the loss of water (including toilets) and electricity.

- Stay warm and dry. If it's cold weather, put on extra layers of clothing; ensure that feet, hands and head are kept warm. Wrap up in blankets or duvets. If you have a fireplace, store dry firewood or other fuel in advance.

EVACUATION

If you do have to leave your home in the case of such events as an earthquake or flooding:

- Turn off the water and electricity supplies to your property. Only shut off the gas if you need to as a professional may need to be brought in to turn it back on.

If your home is at risk of flooding, move household items out of the reach of flood-waters and have tarpaulins on hand to help keep your belongings dry. Think about having sandbags ready to use. But if the situation is dire don't wait for any official notice of evacuation – just GO!

- Disconnect all electrical appliances.
- Advise friends and family of your meeting point.
- Move all vehicles that may be in the way of emergency vehicles.
- Have grab bags ready for everyone in your household.
- Lock your home.
- If your situation is dire don't wait for any official notice of evacuation – **just GO!**
- If your home is at risk of flooding, move household items out of the reach of flood-waters and have tarpaulins on hand to help keep your belongings dry. Think about having sandbags ready to use.

IF IN DOUBT, GET OUT!

SHELTER

EMERGENCY SHELTER

If you have to leave your home, your focus must quickly shift to alternative shelter options for you and your household, such as staying with friends or family or in motels, camping grounds, emergency shelters or even your car.

Tents can be your first port of call as they can be quickly set up in your garden. If you don't have a tent, then you can quickly set up an emergency shelter using a tarpaulin and some rope or cord. Tie the rope or cord between 2 poles or trees and lay the tarpaulin over it. On the ground under the tarpaulin, put down any insulating material you can find (such as sheets of cardboard or leafy tree branches) to provide a barrier between you and the ground. This will help you stay dry and warm.

Your car can also be a temporary shelter in an emergency if nowhere else is available. You can extend the space available by adding a canopy extension from 1 or both sides of the car using a tarpaulin as an awning – run the tarpaulin from the top of the car to poles supported by guy ropes, tie these to tree branches or use tent pegs to keep the ropes tight.

PROMPTS

- If it looks like it's safest to evacuate, don't wait – **just GO!**
- If you've ever done any camping you're halfway there when it comes to emergency tent life.
- Include with your household emergency supply kit a roll of heavy-duty plastic sheeting or tarpaulins, a hammer and nails, duct tape, lengths of wood and cord, all of which will be very useful in making temporary repairs to your house, such as covering broken windows or areas where roof tiles or roofing iron have blown off.
- If staying in your home, fill up baths, sinks and containers with water as insurance against the water supply being affected.
- If you are using a generator, the generator must be placed in an outdoor location where the exhaust will not collect or cause carbon monoxide poisoning. Small generators can be used to power lights and small appliances, even a refrigerator or freezer. Power stations are more easily used although these tend to have a lesser electrical supply.

FOOD AND WATER

The most helpful action you can take in preparing your household for an emergency is to put together a store of food and water. You may be prevented from getting to the grocery store by road closures or even if you can get there, damage to transport networks may have affected food distribution. Whatever the reason, you'll be thankful that you have your own stash of food and water to call on if an emergency does happen.

Work towards building up a reserve of, at minimum, 1 week's supply of emergency food — foodstuffs that don't need refrigeration, cooking or much water to prepare. If you like, building up your emergency stock can be done gradually and more affordably by purchasing items 1 or 2 at a time on your usual weekly shop.

If you have integrated the emergency supply with your everyday pantry stock, then it's important to rotate your emergency stock so that it doesn't expire before you need to use it. Keeping your supply of emergency foodstuffs in a separate part of the pantry, or in a separate location, prevents you from accidentally using it all as part of your normal food supply.

Once established, the emergency food and water supplies should be regularly used and replenished — so that foods are used while they are still within best-by dates and you maintain the emergency quantity.

STORING FOOD

Aim for foods high in calories, protein, carbohydrates, vitamins and minerals. Look for canned foods with high liquid content in case water is scarce. Look for long lasting food that doesn't need cooking — unless you have a camping stove and fuel for a barbecue — as electricity and gas may not be available. Remember to have a mechanical can opener for canned food.

Suggested foodstuffs to stock up include:

- Ready-to-eat canned meats, fruits and vegetables.
- Canned juice, long-life or powdered milk and soup. Pre-packaged beverages (those in foil packets and foil-lined boxes are sealed and will keep for a long time if the seal is not broken).
- High-energy foods such as peanut butter, jam, salt-free crackers and energy bars.
- Scroggin or trail mix (pre-packaged or homemade).
- Comfort foods such as sweetened cereals, snack bars and biscuits.
- Instant coffee and tea bags.
- Dried or bulk foods like dried fruit, nuts or crackers — also pasta, rice and dried beans. Avoid very salty foods, as they may increase thirst.
- Freeze-dried foods. They are tasty and lightweight but will need water for reconstitution.
- Whole-grain cereals (oatmeal, whole-wheat, multi-grain).

- Instant meals. Cups of noodles or cups of soup are an effective addition, although they need water for reconstitution.
- Snack-sized canned goods, which generally have pull-top lids or twist-open keys.
- Foods for infants, elderly persons or persons on special diets.
- Non-perishable foods for pets.

CONSIDERATIONS REGARDING EMERGENCY FOOD

Keep in mind that commercially dehydrated foods will require water to prepare; whole grains, beans and dried pasta also require water for preparation and cooking. It's ideal to prep other food options as well, as water can be in short supply in an emergency.

A power outage will mean that refrigerated and frozen food faces spoilage. Food in your fridge is safe for up to 4 hours after the electricity goes off while food in a freezer can last from 1–2 days depending on if the freezer is half full (1 day) or completely full: the greater thermal mass of the full freezer provides longer temperature retention.

Keep an eye on shelf life: most foodstuffs can be safely eaten beyond their 'use by' or 'best before' dates; canned foods generally for 2–5 years, carton foods such as breakfast cereals can still be okay for 6 months after the 'best by' date. Check food before eating and throw away anything that smells bad and any tins that are dented or bulging. Store foodstuffs in a cool, dry and dark place.

If you're evacuating on foot, you won't want to be carrying a heavy load of canned food. Opt instead for powdered soups, instant noodles and dehydrated meals (the latter are not just tasty but also nutritious thanks, in part, to food preservation research by NASA). But remember you will need to have access to sufficient water to make these.

For ease of moving your emergency food supply, store it in bags, cartons or crates, which will also make it easier to handle and pack into your car if you have to relocate.

FOOD SUPPLIES — SAFETY AND SANITATION

A few dos and don'ts to ensure hygienic handling of your emergency food:

Do:

- Keep food in covered containers.
- Keep cooking and eating utensils clean.
- Keep garbage in closed containers and dispose outside, burying it if necessary.
- Discard any food that has come into contact with contaminated flood-water.
- Thawed food can usually be eaten if it is still 'refrigerator cold' and can be re-frozen if it still contains ice crystals.

Don't:

- Eat foods from cans that are swollen, dented or corroded, even if the product looks safe to eat.
- Let garbage accumulate inside, for reason of both fire-risk and good sanitation.

WHEN IN DOUBT, THROW IT OUT

MEAL PREPARATION

Alternative cooking options in times of emergency include fireplaces, barbecues and camping stoves. Commercially canned food may be eaten out of the can without warming. If heating canned food, open it before heating.

Do not use outdoor gas appliances such as patio heaters, camp cookers and barbecues indoors. These appliances do not have safety systems in place that will shut off the gas supply when oxygen levels are depleted and high levels of carbon monoxide are present. Carbon monoxide is a highly poisonous gas. Prolonged or high-level exposure can cause collapse, unconsciousness and even death. Breathing small amounts of carbon monoxide can cause headaches, nausea, dizziness, tiredness and vomiting. If you suspect you have been exposed to carbon monoxide, immediately move into fresh air and seek medical attention. If it can be done safely, turn off the appliance and ventilate the room.

Depending on how much food you have stored and the duration of the emergency event, you may find yourself having to economise on meals to make your store of food last longer, for example:

- An 800g packet of rolled oats will make a large number of bowls of porridge and give people a nutritious and warming start to the day (porridge can be cooked quickly by simply pouring boiling water over the oats in your breakfast bowl; no need for a pot or a stove).
- A 400g tin of baked beans can provide the basis of 2 nutritional meals. A dozen tins, then, is an emergency meal stash large enough to supply 2 people with 2 meals a day for a week. Baked beans – as with most canned food – can be eaten straight from the tin

without needing to be heated. If you're not keen on baked beans daily — and cold beans at that — it's good to remember that they are a great source of protein and better than nothing in an emergency. They can be mixed into other foods such as rice or potatoes if you have those.

- Sprouted beans, legumes and microgreens can act as a fresh 'vegetable' in the event of an emergency. A packet of dried mung beans goes a long way. Place a few tablespoons of the mung beans in a wide glass jar or similar and cover with water, leaving to soak overnight. Drain off the water in the morning. In the evening, rinse and drain the beans as before, repeating this the next morning as well. By the second evening the beans will be sufficiently sprouted to eat. If you prefer longer sprouted stems, continue the process for another day.
- If you need to start a fire but it's wet and damp, fire starter tablets used with barbecues will help. Or you can invest in a flint striker from an outdoors store.

If the power goes out, eat the food from your fridge first, then from your freezer. Then eat the food in the cupboard or in your emergency supply kit.

STORING WATER

Water is the most essential emergency supply. Generally, 3 litres of water per day per person is recommended based on normal activity. If it's hot, however, or you're working hard, then you need to increase that. Store at least a 3-day supply of water, so 9 litres per person for the 3 days. This will be enough for drinking requirements (3 litres per day per person) plus water for basic hygiene. You will need to store more for cleaning.

In an emergency, water supplies can be interrupted or its safety and availability compromised: water mains may be broken or contaminated by the outflow from damaged sewers. A major emergency may see water supplies out for weeks if not months. Plan your emergency water supply accordingly and make sure you have enough — commercially-bottled water, or your own containers filled from the tap — available.

Store more if you can. Hot environments and intense physical activity can double the amount required. Children, nursing mothers and people who are ill will also need more water. Be sure to also include drinking and clean-up water for your pets.

A 200-litre emergency water tank of the kind that can be connected to a downpipe on your home for collecting rainwater.

PREPARING CONTAINERS OF WATER

If you choose to fill your own storage containers, choose large plastic soft drink or fruit juice bottles, not plastic jugs or cardboard containers that have had milk in them. (Milk protein cannot be adequately removed from these containers and will provide an environment for bacterial growth. Cardboard containers also leak easily and are not designed for long-term storage of liquids.) Don't use glass containers as they can break and are heavy. When storing water:

1	Thoroughly clean the containers and lids with hot water (not boiling, as this will damage the bottle).
2	Fill the containers with regular tap water until it overflows, then replace the bottle cap.
3	Tightly close the containers using the original caps, making sure there are no air gaps. Be careful not to contaminate the caps by touching the inside of them with your fingers.
4	With a permanent marker, write the date on the outside of the containers so that you know when you filled them and when to refresh them.
5	Store in a cool, dark place.
6	Check the bottles every 6 months, easily remembered if you do this at the beginning and end of daylight saving. If the water is not clear, throw it out and repeat steps 2 to 5 with fresh water.
7	If you have commercially bottled water, replace it as per its expiration date.

If you're using food-grade water storage containers, before filling with water, thoroughly clean the containers with dishwashing soap and water, then rinse completely so there is no residual soap. Follow the given steps when filling the containers with water. For ease of use, choose storage containers that have a spigot or tap on the side.

Six 1.5-litre bottles will provide sufficient water for 1 person for 3 days during a water supply outage.

EMERGENCY SOURCES OF WATER

- In an emergency, water can be obtained from various places within your home, such as the hot water cylinder and toilet cisterns. Water from toilet cisterns is only safe to use if no chemical toilet cleaner is present. Bail out water from the toilet cistern using a cup and boil for 1 minute before drinking. Access the water in your hot water cylinder by turning on a hot water tap.
- To use the water in your hot water tank, be sure the electricity or gas is off. Refill the tank before turning the gas or electricity back on.
- Rainwater can be collected by placing a clean container outside to catch rain or by disconnecting the downpipe from the roof and filling a container. If you have nothing

else, you can form a 'funnel' using a clean plastic tarpaulin. Boil any water you collect for 1 minute before drinking.

- Water storage tanks can be connected to downpipes to collect rainwater or used to store tap water. Before purchasing, check with your local council to see if there are any planning requirements you need to consider.
- Two-storey houses with upstairs plumbing will hold a few litres of water in the pipes. To access this water, open a tap upstairs to break the vacuum seal then turn on a tap downstairs and collect the water as it drains out of the pipes. There is water available in both the hot- and cold-water pipes. If the mains water supply has not been contaminated, this water is safe to drink.
- You can also fill plastic ice cream containers with water and keep them in the freezer. These can help keep frozen food cool if the power is off and the water resulting from the melted ice can be used for drinking.

TREATING CONTAMINATED WATER

There may be situations where water is available but is not considered safe for human consumption. This can occur after repairs have been made to the municipal water supplies, water has been obtained from questionable sources or water is being pulled from storage containers after a long time.

Treat all water of uncertain quality before using it for drinking, food washing or preparation, washing dishes, brushing teeth or making ice. In addition to having a bad odour and taste, contaminated water can contain microorganisms that cause diseases such as dysentery, cholera, typhoid and hepatitis. There are several ways to treat water. None is perfect; often the best solution is a combination of methods.

Below are a few methods that can help to ensure your water is safe to drink. Your water will need to be clear before starting. If the water is cloudy, filter it first through a clean cloth, paper towel or coffee filter, and allow to settle, before drawing off the clear water for treatment as follows:

- Boiling is the safest method of treating water. In a large pot or kettle, bring water to a boil for 1 full minute, keeping in mind that some water will evaporate. Let the water cool before drinking. Boiled water will taste better if you put oxygen back into it by pouring the water back and forth between 2 clean containers. (This technique will also improve the taste of stored water.)
- Chlorination uses household liquid bleach to kill microorganisms. Do not use scented bleaches, colour safe bleaches or bleaches with added cleaners. See Civil Defence guidelines for preparation.
- While boiling and chlorinating water will kill most microbes, distillation will remove the microbes that resist these methods, as well as heavy metals, salts and most other chemicals. Distillation involves boiling the water and then collecting the vapour that condenses, leaving behind salts and other impurities. To distil, fill a pot halfway with water. Tie a cup to the handle on the pot's lid so that the cup will hang right-side-up when the lid is upside-down (make sure the cup is not dangling into the water). Place the pot lid upside down on top of the pot and boil the water for 20 minutes. The water that drips from the lid into the cup will be distilled.
- Commercial water filters can also be purchased.

PROMPTS

- If you or someone in your household has special dietary needs, make sure you have sufficient stock of these food items for a minimum of 3 days, or ideally a week or more if you can.
- Drink according to your needs. Many people need more than the average of 2 litres per day (the individual amount needed depends on age, physical activity, physical condition and time of year). Drink the amount you need today and try to find more for tomorrow. Under no circumstances should a person drink less than 4 cups of water each day.
- Do not drink carbonated, caffeinated or alcoholic beverages as a replacement for drinking water. Carbonated beverages do not meet drinking-water requirements and caffeinated drinks and alcohol dehydrate the body, which increases the need for drinking water.
- Remember to pack a mechanical can opener with your emergency food supplies.
- Put together a list of recipes for 1-pot meals.
- Commercially tinned food is able to be eaten straight out of the can without heating.
- Supplement meals with fresh foods if you can.
- Dehydrated commercial food kits or one-off meals have the advantage of being ready-made and lightweight.
- Store supplies in sturdy, easy to carry containers such as backpacks, duffle bags or covered rubbish containers.

- Ensure healthy food handling habits, storing food in covered containers. Wash your hands frequently. Dispose of rubbish outside away from living quarters
- Check your stored water every 6 months. If the water isn't clear, throw it out, clean the bottles thoroughly and refill.

UTILITIES

Following an emergency event check your household utilities (electricity, gas and water) and if these are damaged it may be necessary to turn them off. Emergency service providers and utility employees will be overwhelmed following a disaster, so it is important that those in your household know when and how to shut off your water and electricity as well as gas if you have to.

> **WITHOUT THE ELECTRICITY GRID, LIFE AS WE KNOW IT CHANGES IN AN INSTANT. ARE YOU PREPARED FOR THAT?**

If the electricity grid fails, it's not just your lights that go out, it's also your water supply, doing the laundry, heating your home and cooking meals (unless you're on gas and the event has spared that energy source). Loss of electricity will also impact electronic financial transactions and access to ATMs. Have some cash on hand at all times, and when the power goes out you'll still be able to pay for groceries.

Think about backup/replacement power and accessories such as:

- A solar panel for recharging devices.
- Gas camping stove and spare gas cannisters.
- A generator or power station.
- Battery-powered radio.
- Torches and spare batteries – or a rechargeable torch.

ELECTRICITY SHUT OFF

Make sure everyone in your household knows how to turn off the electricity at the mains switchboard inside your home in the event of an emergency. It's recommended that you first turn off individual appliances including the fridge and freezer (keep fridge and freezer doors closed) before switching the main switch to the OFF position.

GENERATORS AND POWER STATIONS

During an electricity outage, replacement electricity can be provided by a generator or power station, allowing you to run lights and various appliances.

Portable generators, unlike backup generators, do not require professional installation and are available in a range of power outputs; smaller units capable of running only a limited number of electrical appliances and larger units, which may be less portable, which will be able to run most, if not all, of a household's demand. Typically, portable generators are fuelled by petrol, although some might run on diesel. They are often used as an emergency power source for large appliances such as refrigerators, or as a general power source for those living in remote parts of the country where mains electricity supply isn't an option. Generators tend to be heavy and noisy. They also emit carbon monoxide (CO), which is a poisonous gas. They should never be used indoors and should be kept many metres away from the house. Do not connect generators to your home's electrical system to prevent energising the electrical lines. Failure to isolate the generator from the power grid puts repair workers at risk of electrocution.

Portable power stations work well with lighter loads. Since portable power stations run on batteries and have a lower power output, they tend to be smaller than generators but can fit a variety of situations and are frequently used during power outages to keep the lights on as well as mobile phones and other devices charged. They are generally lighter and more compact than generators and have the benefit of being almost silent during operation. As the batteries drain, a portable power station must be recharged, by mains electricity if that's available or solar panels. You will not be able to use it while it recharges.

The choice between a generator and a portable power station comes down to what you need it for. If you need something portable with low power output, go with a portable power station. If you need a higher output and continuous power, a generator will run continuously, as long as you have fuel.

USING A GENERATOR DURING POWER OUTAGES

Don't overload your generator: determine the amount of power you will need to operate those things you plan to connect to and make sure your generator produces more power than will be drawn (including the initial surge when it is turned on). If your generator doesn't produce enough power to operate everything at once, stagger the use of your equipment, otherwise you may trip the overload protection on the generator or damage the connected equipment. When setting up a generator, there are a few things you need to keep in mind:

- Keep your generator outdoors, and place it away from windows, doors and vents. To avoid electrocution, keep the generator dry and avoid touching it with wet hands. Do not use in wet conditions. Operate it on a dry surface under an open canopy-like structure.
- Use and store generator fuel safely. Turn the generator off and let it cool before refuelling. Gasoline spilled on hot engine parts could ignite. If you spill fuel or do not seal its container properly, invisible vapours can travel along the ground and be ignited by an appliance's pilot light or arcs from electric switches in the appliance.
- Plug appliances directly into the generator, or use a heavy duty, outdoor-rated extension cord that is rated (in watts or amps) at least equal to the sum of the connected appliance loads.
- Never try to power your house wiring by plugging the generator into a wall outlet, a practice known as 'back feeding'. It can lead to the electrocution of utility workers or neighbours served by the same utility transformer. The only safe way to connect a generator to a house is to have a qualified electrician install a power transfer switch.

THEN THERE'S YOUR ELECTRIC CAR . . .

That car parked in the drive is not only personal transport, but it can also act as a personal power station.

Electric vehicles (EVs) are essentially batteries on wheels. If your EV — either full electric or hybrid — is equipped with something called vehicle-to-grid or vehicle-to-home technology, it can be used to keep the lights on in an emergency event. This technology allows the power from your battery to be transferred into your home or into the grid.

Average EV batteries hold more than 60 kilowatt hours (kWh) of energy, enough to provide backup power to an average New Zealand household for 2 days. An EV with bidirectional charging is the easiest way to power the entire house. Bidirectional charging means electricity can be drawn from the grid and put back into the grid. Not all EVs have this capability, so it's important to check first if you intend to use your battery this way.

Some Kiwis used their electric vehicle batteries in this way to help power essential home appliances following the January 2023 weather bomb and Cyclone Gabrielle. When Cyclone Gabrielle hit the North Island, 46,000 households lost power. Some homes were without power for days, and despite the increasing uptake of solar power, very few households had a backup power source to run their basic appliances on. To power your home with an EV battery, you'll need an inverter that can be connected to individual appliances with extension leads. Or, for a more permanent set-up, you'll need a home integration system that allows the power from your battery to be converted into usable power for your house. Currently, home integration systems aren't readily available in New Zealand. Some homeowners, however, are getting past this hurdle by having a system installed that enables them to switch from mains power to backup power generation simply by flicking a switch on their mains switchboard.

The usefulness of this setup was exemplified in 2021 when an ice storm left millions of Texans without electricity. Ford in the United States had recently released a hybrid version of its F-150 truck, which essentially doubles as a generator, sporting as many as 11 outlets spread around the vehicle, including a 240-volt outlet, and during the storm, Ford dealers lent out several of the F-150s as home generators. Instead of plugging appliances into the truck, the truck plugs into the house, replacing the grid. An 80-amp bidirectional charger and home integration system is used, allowing a house to be disconnected from the grid and powered by the F-150 instead.

During power cuts over the last 6 years, West Auckland resident Jonathan Beaver has been powering his house directly from the battery of his 2011 Nissan Leaf via a 12V inverter and has taken the step of getting the system integrated with his switchboard. During Cyclone Gabrielle, Jonathan's power lines were knocked over by trees, leaving him without power for 7 days and his system proved its worth. 'It's extremely easy to use. You either switch onto "mains" and everything runs normally, or you switch on "generator" and that automatically isolates everything as well as connecting the generator input, which in this case, is connected to the inverter, which is connected to the car.'

When there is a mains outage, Jonathan can use this system to keep the lights, fridge and freezer on, keep phones and laptops charged, as well as the water pump and wastewater systems running. The only downside to using the 12-volt inverter is that it can only supply low power loads up to a total of 1000 watts and requires turning a number of appliances off before switching over to EV battery power.

If you don't own an EV, you can still make use of your regular car's battery as a source of power. For example, it can power a string of lights for inside your house. Position your car as close as possible to a window into your house and connect a string of 12-volt lights to the battery (attach the ends of the light's wires to battery clips for easy connection). Instant lighting in an emergency!

EMERGENCY GAS SHUT OFF

Avoid turning off piped gas supplies to your house unless absolutely necessary as any closed-off supply requires a professional to reconnect. On a regular day this wouldn't be a problem, but following a big emergency, individual homes will be low priority for trade professionals. You could be without gas service for several days or much longer. However, if you do smell gas or hear a leak then it's vital that you do turn off the gas.

Everyone in your household should know where the gas meter is located and how to turn it off in an emergency – consult your supplier's website for more information. Most meters are at the front or side of the house. Some are put inside the building. In apartments or commercial buildings, they might be in the back.

WATER SHUT OFF

Water becomes a precious resource following a big emergency; teaching everyone in the household how to turn off the water is important. Unlike gas, water can be turned on and off with no safety concerns.

Water lines into the house could leak or burst following an emergency event or could be polluted from cracked main water pipes. Following a major event that could have caused pipe breakages, it's a good idea to turn off the water until you hear from authorities that the water supply is safe.

Locate the shut-off valve (known as a toby) — it's usually inside a box on the perimeter of your property, near where the water supply enters; for most houses this will most likely be on the front boundary. Make sure that the valve can be completely shut off, turning it clockwise. Check that your toby is not jammed open and that it closes fully. If it is stuck or only partially closes, fix those problems and ensure it shuts off completely.

If you're notified of a planned outage, keep buckets of water nearby on the day for flushing the toilet. Fill up the bath as well.

Turn off the water supply to your house following an emergency if you think there could be a pipe breakage in order to stop leaks and to prevent the household supply being polluted. The shut-off valve is usually inside a box on the perimeter of your property.

POWER SHUT OFF

No power? Log a fault with your electricity retailer — that's the company you pay your power bill to — and check their website to see if there are any details of outages.

- Keep a torch (battery or rechargeable), battery-powered lantern and spare batteries handy. Battery-powered lights are safer than candles and matches.
- You can buy small USB light sticks that fit into the USB slot on a power pack, the kind used to recharge mobile phones. This will provide hours of bright light.
- Another source of room lighting is solar-powered garden lights. Charge these up outside during the day, then bring them inside at night to light up rooms in the house.
- Switch off and unplug sensitive electronic appliances such as computers and TVs. These can be affected by a power surge when the electricity comes back on. Surge protection devices can also be used to protect electronic appliances from damage. If you experience a power surge, switch appliances off at the wall. If a power surge affects your appliances or internal wiring, contact your retailer.
- It's a good idea to check that stove elements and heaters are also turned off, this will ensure they don't come back on without you noticing when the electricity is restored. Leave on an overhead light so you'll know when the power is back on.
- Keep your fridge and freezer closed. Most freezers will keep food at a safe temperature for 1–2 days depending on how full it is and as long as the door stays closed.
- Make sure you fully charge your devices regularly and consider having a spare battery or mobile power pack on hand.

- Know how to override electric-opening garage doors in the event of an outage. With many garage door openers there is a cord to the front of the motor. Pull this down until it clicks then push up the garage door by hand.
- Unplug appliances ahead of an electrical storm. If the power goes out, turn off appliances in use, such as heaters, stove tops, kettles and ovens so they don't come on straight away when the power returns as this could overload the system.
- Label the mains switch on your switchboard (if it isn't already readily identifiable) so you can quickly turn off the power when you have to.
- If you or someone in your household is medically dependent on an electrical device, it's important to check with your/their doctor and your energy retailer to create a backup plan.
- One of the most common causes of electricity outages during a storm is from trees or branches falling on power lines. Ensure that trees on your property and those planted on the berms are kept clear of power lines.

EMERGENCY TOILETS

In an emergency event, there will be things we do in our daily lives that we'll have to adjust our approach to toilets, for example. If an earthquake, or other event results in broken sewer lines or broken water mains you won't be able to use your toilet and will need alternatives in place ready to go.

The 2011 Christchurch earthquake highlighted the vulnerability of sewerage systems to disruption during an earthquake and the lengthy restoration time involved. It showed how vital it is that we plan for such disruptions and for individuals and communities to be prepared to manage their toilet waste.

Toilet systems can be impaired because of broken pipes, flooding or a breakdown of pumping systems. In any of these situations, and if your toilet can't be used, you're going to need a makeshift alternative. Even if the water is still running, there's a chance that wastewater pipes will be broken, in which case if the toilet was flushed, its contents could end up in your – or your neighbour's – garden!

NO RUNNING WATER MEANS NO FLUSHING TOILETS

The wastewater network (which takes away the water we pour down the sink, and our toilet waste) is even more vulnerable than the drinking water network — its broken pipes take longer to find and fix, and there are more of them. If there are lengthy outages to the wastewater systems in your region, you may be unable to flush your toilet for months and should be prepared to deal with the disposal of your toilet waste for some time.

Following the Christchurch earthquake, Massey University led a collaboration with Wellington Water, National Public Health/Te Whatu Ora, Wellington Regional Emergency Management Office (WREMO) and the Wellington region's 8 councils, along with stakeholders from Ngāti Toa, the disability sector and managers and contractors of solid waste to develop an emergency sanitation plan.

Two viable options were offered: making a long drop or a two-bucket toilet system (1 for urine and 1 for faeces). The plan also includes an option for those with accessibility needs or limited mobility.

Until the widespread development of water-flushed sewage systems, long drops were commonplace in rural and urban settlements. Even today, this simple, hole-in-the-ground privy can be found in New Zealand's more rural areas and in some of its basic camping grounds.

At its simplest the long drop is just a deep hole in the ground. A raised board with a hole in it set across the top acts as the toilet seat. When the existing long drop is full you fill it in with earth and dig a new one. Although mostly of the simplest utilitarian design and construction, there were practical and even aesthetic considerations to be taken into account. As described in the 1929 book *The Specialist* by Charles Sale, the story's main character Lem Put, a rural carpenter specialising in building outhouses, outlines some of the important points when creating a long drop:

> Now, about the diggin' of her. You can't be too careful about that, dig her deep and dig her wide. It's a mighty sight better to have a little privy over a big hole than a big privy over a little hole. Another thing; when you dig her deep you've got 'er dug; and you ain't got that disconcertin' thought stealin' over you that sooner or later you'll have to dig again.
>
> As to the latch fer her, I can give you a spool and string, or a hook and eye. The cost of a spool and string is practically nothin' but they ain't positive in action. If somebody comes out and starts rattlin' the door, either the spool or the string is apt to give way, and there you are. But, with a hook and eye she's yours, you might say, for the whole afternoon, if you're so minded. Put on the hook and eye of the best quality 'cause there ain't nothin' that'll rack a man's nerves more than to be sittin' there ponderin', without a good, strong, substantial latch on the door.

If you can't build a long drop, the two-bucket system can easily be set up in your bathroom or other area of your house. Urine is generally sterile and as such it can be safely disposed of into your garden. Faeces, however, contains bacteria that can cause a number of illnesses and requires careful management and disposal. The two-bucket system means that urine and faeces can be kept separate, resulting in a lower volume of excreta needing to be handled as well as minimising the smell.

HOW TO BUILD AN EMERGENCY TOILET

OPTION 1. BUILD A LONG DROP

You will need:

- Backyard or space on your property to dig a large hole.
- Tools to dig a hole.
- Soil or other fill/mulch such as straw, sawdust or shredded newspaper.

Dig a hole up to 1 metre deep and 30–40cm wide. Make sure the hole is away from any water source, above the groundwater table and far away from any vegetable gardens. This hole can also be used to hold solid waste from a bucket toilet.

To make a seat for the long drop:

- Cut a hole in the base of a plastic garden chair and place the chair over your long drop. If you like, the toilet seat from your house toilet can be unscrewed and attached to the garden chair.
- You can also build a wooden box frame with a toilet seat to go over the long drop hole. The wooden box frame should be strong enough to support users and easy to clean (painting or varnishing it will help).

After each use, cover with soil or other fill/mulch. Keep the hole covered after using, for hygiene and safety reasons.

You can do this by placing a piece of board or heavy-duty cardboard over the hole, this will discourage pests or pets from getting into the long drop.

When the waste gets to 30cm below the surface, it's time to fill the hole. Cover the hole with soil and dig yourself a new long drop.

For the sake of privacy, you could erect a framework of poles around the long drop and wrap a tarpaulin around them with a second tarpaulin tied across the top. Or use some old wooden pallets to make a wooden screen.

OPTION 2. MAKE AN EMERGENCY BUCKET TOILET

You will need:

- Two sturdy 15–20-litre buckets with lids.
- Permanent marker (to label the buckets).
- Dry mulch such as sawdust, dry leaves and soil or shredded newspaper.
- Water – 2 litres of water per person, per day.

Set up your 2 buckets in your normal bathroom or laundry. With a permanent marker, label bucket 1 with 'urine' and bucket 2 with 'faeces'. It is important that you try to keep your urine and faeces separate as this will help keep the smell down and make handling the waste safer. If you have a garage, setting the bucket toilets there would make it easier to take buckets into the garden for emptying, and to clean up any spills.

To make a seat:

You can make a seat for your bucket toilet using 2 planks of wood laid across the top, using a pool noodle (see picture on page 140), or by placing a toilet seat atop the bucket.

You can make a more comfortable seat using a plastic garden chair or by creating a wooden box frame.

- Cut a hole in the base of a plastic garden chair and place the chair over your bucket toilet. If you like, the toilet seat from your house toilet can be unscrewed and attached to the garden chair.
- You can also build a wooden box frame with a toilet seat to go over the bucket toilet. The wooden box frame should be strong enough to support users and easy to clean (painting or varnishing it will help).

BUCKET 1 (urine):

- This bucket should be for urine only (place any toilet paper used into bucket 2). Add 2–3 cm of water to the bottom of your clean bucket before use.
- Once you have used the bucket, replace the lid on top and wash your hands.

Disposing of your urine

At the end of each day, dilute your urine with a little more water and pour it into a disused area of your garden.

BUCKET 2 (faeces):

- Add a layer of dry mulch (sawdust, straw, dry leaves, soil or shredded newspaper) to the bottom of your clean bucket. Use this bucket for faeces and toilet paper only. You do not need to line the bucket with a bag if you have garden space to dispose of the contents. If you do not have a garden or green space, line your faeces bucket with a sturdy bin liner/bag before use.
- When you have finished, add a large cup or handful of dry mulch to cover your faeces. This helps to keep the smell down and break down the faeces.
- Replace the lid on top of the bucket and wash your hands.

- Try to keep the faeces bucket as dry as possible. Sometimes it's hard to go without urinating as well but if you can keep the 2 wastes separate, then this will keep the smell down and make it safer to handle. Use the sawdust, straw or shredded newspaper to absorb any spills.
- Menstrual cups should be emptied into this bucket. Period products and nappies go in a normal rubbish bin.

Disposing of your faeces

Bucket 2 will need to be emptied at least every 3 days.

- If you have a garden or green space, dig a 50cm hole in the ground and empty the contents of bucket 2 into it.
- If you do not have a garden or green space, line your faeces bucket with a sturdy bin liner/bag before use. When you have finished, add a large cup or handful of dry mulch to cover your faeces. Then replace the bucket lid and wash your hands.
- Dispose of the faeces bag from bucket 2 in a large storage bin, e.g., a wheelie bin or other outdoor lidded bin.

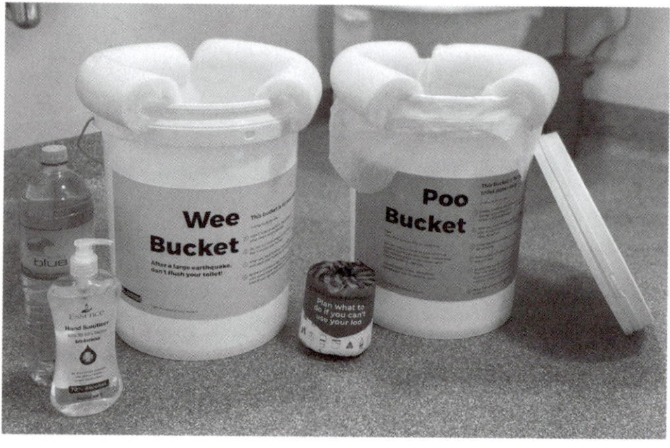

The two-bucket emergency toilet solution. Wrapping something soft around the tops of the buckets – such as the pool noodle seen here – will make the buckets more comfortable to sit on.

- Wear gloves and rinse and clean the faeces bucket after emptying. Disinfect with a dilute bleach solution if necessary.
- If you live in an apartment with a communal rubbish skip bin, put your faeces bag in there.
- Try to keep the faeces bucket as dry as possible. Use the sawdust, straw or shredded newspaper to absorb any spills.

WHY SEPARATE FAECES AND URINE?

Keeping faeces and urine separate reduces the smell. It is also safer, as urine contains far fewer germs than faeces. By keeping urine and faeces separate, you will find that your bucket toilets are easier to empty and more hygienic. During an emergency, it is very important to minimise the spread of diseases. Human faeces contain a lot of dangerous germs, and so a hygienic system for your emergency toilet will help your household avoid getting sick.

OPTIONS FOR THOSE WITH ACCESSIBILITY NEEDS OR LIMITED MOBILITY

These options should only be used for those with accessibility needs or limited mobility and for whom the long drop or two-bucket emergency toilet is not feasible.

- Look into the option of a commode chair. If it has a pail, place a sturdy plastic bag or bin liner inside.
- A last resort option is to place a large, sturdy bin liner/ plastic bag inside your toilet bowl. The bag needs to be big enough to cover the whole bowl to avoid spillage. Place some dry material in the bag such as sawdust, straw, dry leaves, soil or shredded newspaper, to soak up as much urine as possible. Dispose of the bag into an outdoor rubbish bin.
- Make sure you clean your hands thoroughly.

HOW TO MAKE AN EMERGENCY TOILET IF YOU LIVE IN AN APARTMENT:

- Use two buckets discussed previously (1 for urine and 1 for faeces).
- Line your faeces bucket with a sturdy bin liner/bag.
- In your faeces bucket, when you have finished, add a large cup or handful of dry mulch (sawdust, kitty litter, straw, dry leaves, soil or shredded newspaper) to cover your faeces. Then close the lid and wash your hands.
- Try to keep the faeces bucket as dry as possible. Sometimes it's hard to go without urine coming out, but if you can keep them separate, then this will keep the smell down and make it safer to handle. Use mulch materials such as sawdust, straw or shredded newspaper to absorb any spills.

DISPOSING OF YOUR URINE AND FAECES

- Dilute your urine and empty into a green space outside.
- Your faeces bucket will need to be emptied at least every 3 days or more frequently. Put your faeces bag in your normal apartment skip bin. Discuss with the other people in your apartment complex to make sure that everyone keeps to the highest levels of cleanliness and health protection.

ALWAYS WASH HANDS BEFORE PREPARING MEALS AND BEFORE EATING

Without clean running water and a functioning sewer system there is greater likelihood of diarrheal disease outbreaks. Good personal hygiene is vital. After using the toilet, wash your hands thoroughly using soap and water, or use hand sanitiser. Dry your hands thoroughly.

Set up a hand-washing station with a large water container with a spigot, soap or hand sanitiser and hand towels – make sure everyone in your household washes their hands after dealing with toilet waste and before preparing food.

Alternatively, a water bottle with a sport top can be used for washing and rinsing hands. Keep the outside of the water bottle clean by using a paper towel to hold it. Or ask someone to squirt the water from the bottle while you are washing/rinsing.

CHEMICAL TOILETS AND PORTALOOS

The use of portaloos and chemical toilets during an emergency poses problems in terms of the storage, collection and treatment: road access to your property could be unavailable and municipal treatment plants may not be able to treat chemical waste at the time.

WHAT IF I HAVE A SEPTIC TANK?

If you have a septic tank, and you are confident that it is still operational and that the drainage field is not impacted, you can still use it. If there is damage to either the tank or the drainage field, avoid use and contact a drainlayer.

WASTEWATER ISN'T JUST ABOUT TOILETS

You'll also need to think about how you will dispose of water used for cooking and hygiene. Water from cooking can be tipped into gardens. Water used for washing clothes or your person should be kept away from vegetable gardens.

EMERGENCY ALTERNATIVES FOR WHEN YOU DON'T HAVE TOILET PAPER!

Toilet paper is something that most of us take for granted. But what happens when there is no toilet paper due to a shortage or an emergency event of some sort?

Modern toilet paper as we know it wasn't invented until the mid-19th century. Before that, people used other things. And we can still use some of these 'other things' now. The Romans, for example, used a sponge that was attached to the end of a stick. As toilets were public, the sponge stick was shared among others using the toilet. When picking up the stick you would want to be careful about which end you picked up . . . the phrase 'getting the wrong end of the stick' is said to derive from when you picked up the wrong end.

Vikings, meanwhile, used discarded pieces of sheep's wool, and the Inuit people are known for using tundra moss or handfuls of snow.

Below are some alternatives for when traditional toilet paper is unavailable:

- Flannel squares, made to around 20cm square. These are soft and convenient to use, and can be washed, dried and reused. Make them yourself out of old pyjamas, sheets, shirts, or other similar fabrics.
- A spray bottle full of water works as a portable bidet and is used to clean yourself after using the toilet. Pick a spray bottle with a decent force to ensure it will do the job.
- Any large plant leaf also works as an alternative to toilet paper. Make sure the type of leaf you are using is not going to cause irritation – avoid leaves with sharp

edges. The large soft leaves of the New Zealand rangiora tree were used by early European settlers, giving rise to the plant's common name 'bushman's toilet paper' and 'bushman's friend'.

- Paper – newspapers, magazines, leaflets, old essays or exams. Cut it up into useful-sized pieces and dampen before use (if the paper is too coarse or rough). Don't try to use glossy paper for obvious reasons.

PROMPTS

- When the toilet cistern won't flush because of a water outage (but the sewer pipes and the toilet itself are otherwise undamaged), you can 'force' a flush yourself, provided you have water saved. Fill a bucket or other container with water and dump it forcefully into the toilet bowl. This should assist in flushing waste down the drain. Repeat as required until the waste has been satisfactorily cleared. In normal circumstances the water that lies in the base of the toilet bowl acts as a 'trap' against unpleasant smells coming up through the toilet. Now, in the absence of a water trap, placing a plastic wrap or plastic bag over the bowl between uses will help to minimise odour.
- Make sure you are emptying and cleaning your toilet buckets regularly. Wash your hands thoroughly using soap and water, or use hand sanitiser, then dry your hands thoroughly after using the toilet, helping children to use the toilet or changing nappies.
- Use gloves when emptying buckets.
- Rinse and clean the faeces bucket after emptying. Disinfect with a diluted bleach solution if necessary.

Continued over page

- Keep the two-bucket toilet set-up and the wastes from it well separated from any food preparation areas.
- If someone does get sick (e.g., is vomiting or has diarrhoea) the rest of the household should use a new separate bucket. Take extra care when emptying the bucket and disinfect with a diluted bleach solution. Seek medical attention for the person if symptoms persist.
- Ready-made bucket toilets with toilet seats can be purchased.

EMERGENCY COMMUNICATIONS

Maintaining telecommunications in an emergency can help prevent loss of life, assist emergency services and ensure that families and local communities can help each other.

When an emergency happens, being able to stay in touch with family and friends and confirm that they are okay is high priority. However, phone and internet communication may be difficult or non-existent if there is loss of electricity, damage to phone lines or cell towers or an overwhelming number of people are trying to get through at the same time. In 2023, when Cyclone Gabrielle wreaked havoc across the North Island, landslips in the East Coast region destroyed fibre optic cables, cutting off communications when cell phone towers lost power.

Fibre and wireless landline connections will stop working if the power goes out. Some cordless phones and other devices, such as medical alarms, may also not be able to connect, even if they have a battery.

Every roadside fibre cabinet and cell phone tower will have an uninterruptible power supply (UPS) of its own that will keep the phone system active for a limited time (hours) until mains power, or power via a generator, can be restored. If systems are moved to generator power, these will only last if fuel is available.

Some people may rely on their fibre or wireless landline to call 111 for health, disability or safety reasons. If this applies to you or someone in your household, ask your provider what they can do to ensure there is a way for you to call 111 in the event of a power cut.

If power is out to the mobile phone system, then your mobile won't work.

PHONING, TEXTING, EMAILING AND OTHER WAYS OF COMMUNICATING IN AN EMERGENCY

The former copper-wire based landline system reliably operated during emergencies and even power cuts as it had its own low-voltage power system. Today, in the age of fibre optic lines and mobile phones, copper landlines are increasingly rare and will soon disappear entirely. Broadband-enabled telephone services will not work during electricity outages without a battery or other backup power source. If you have a battery, test it periodically, understand how long it should last, learn how to replace it and consider having a spare that you can charge before a storm. If you do not have a battery or other backup power source, ask your provider where you can purchase one.

Texting during an emergency event is recommended, to keep phone lines clear for response teams and other urgent communications. If it's vital you make a phone call, keep it brief. Text messages will get through an overloaded telecommunications infrastructure before phone calls.

Email is another option for communication if you can access the internet. If the emails are only text based (i.e., no images) the messages consume very little bandwidth.

Social media can also help you stay connected and create backup pathways for communication. Everyone in the household should be familiar with your household communications plan (see below). Both email and social media communications are, however, dependent on having access to the internet and there being enough bandwidth available.

Two-way radio is another reliable method of communication and, not surprisingly, is the basis of emergency communication within emergency agencies. However, it has limited range.

CREATE A HOUSEHOLD EMERGENCY COMMUNICATION PLAN

This starts with 1 simple question: 'What if?' 'What if something happens and I'm not with my household?' 'How will I be able to reach them?' 'How will I know they are safe?' 'How can I let them know I'm okay?' During an emergency, you will want to be in communication with your household, but, communication networks such as those for mobile phones and computers could be unreliable at this time, while electricity services are disrupted.

Work out a plan that will help ensure all the members of your household know how to reach each other and where to meet up in an emergency event:

1	Create a paper copy of the contact information for each member of your household and other important people/offices, such as medical facilities, doctors, schools and service providers. Ensure everyone carries a copy in their backpack, purse or wallet. You should also put up a copy in a central location in your home, such as on your refrigerator or household bulletin board (if you have one). Having important information written down will help you reconnect with others in case you can't get in touch using your usual means.
2	Make sure all household and emergency contact information is up to date on all household members' mobile phones or devices. Store your details and at least 1 emergency contact under the name 'In Case of Emergency' – or 'ICE' – on all mobile phones and devices. This will help someone identify you and your emergency contacts if needed. Inform your emergency contact of any medical issues or other requirements you may have. Create a group list on all mobile phones and devices of the people you would need to communicate with if there was an emergency.

Because an emergency can strike at any time, including during school and work hours, you need to know the emergency response plans of those entities and how to best stay informed. Discuss these plans with any children in your household and let them know who might pick them up in an emergency. Let your children's school know of any alternative contacts who may pick up your children in the case of an emergency event.

Your household may not be together when an emergency strikes, so plan how you will contact one another. Think about how you will communicate in different situations. Make up a contact card for each household member and have them keep these cards handy in a wallet, purse, backpack. Create a backup by emailing the file to yourself and include a copy in your household emergency supply kit.

EMERGENCY MEETING PLACES

Because it may be impossible to be in contact by phone, sort out a few other safe, familiar places where your household can go for protection or to reunite. Make sure these locations are accessible for household members with disabilities or access and functional needs.

- **In your neighbourhood** – Choose a place in your neighbourhood where your household will meet if there is a fire or other emergency event where you need to leave your home. The meeting place could be a neighbour's house or local park.
- **Outside of your neighbourhood** – This is a place where your household will meet if an emergency happens when you're not at home and can't get back there. This could be a library, community centre, church or a friend's or relative's home.

PREPARING FOR AND DURING AN EMERGENCY

Routinely charge up your mobile phone, laptop or tablet in case of an emergency. Keep a portable power pack and power cord on hand to recharge your mobile phone and other devices when the power goes out.

- A solar panel phone charger that generates 10 watts is usually sufficient for recharging a smartphone over a day. Also, have a charger adapter to charge mobile phones and devices in your car.
- Conserve your mobile phone battery by reducing the brightness of your screen and closing apps you don't need. Avoid watching videos and playing games in order to conserve batteries and to help reduce network congestion.

Limit non-emergency phone calls. This will minimise network congestion and free up 'space' for emergency communications. If you need to make a call, keep it brief and only convey vital information to emergency personnel and/or members of your household. Limiting calls also conserves mobile phone battery power. You can expect mobile phone use to be heavy during and immediately following an emergency event.

Monitor news and emergency broadcasts. Have a battery-powered radio to check news broadcasts for emergency information during power outages. Make sure you have charged or fresh batteries if needed. You can also purchase a solar-powered or hand-cranked radio, which may also be used to charge mobile phones. Make sure household members with phones are signed up for alerts and warnings from their school, workplace and Civil Defence.

Write down the phone numbers of everyone in your household. Having these written down will help you reconnect with others if you don't have your mobile device or computer with you or if the battery runs out. List the numbers of emergency services, utilities, service providers, medical providers, veterinarians, insurance companies and others important to your household.

Make sure everyone, including children, knows when and how to call 111 for help. You should only call 111 if there is a life-threatening emergency.

TRACK HOUSEHOLD MEMBERS VIA YOUR MOBILE PHONE

Your mobile phone can be used to find out the location of family and friends, a useful and maybe even critical ability in an emergency. Go online to find instructions and apps that will allow you to share locations with users of both Android and iPhone mobile phones.

EMERGENCY MOBILE ALERTS

The National Emergency Management Agency (NEMA) is responsible for providing national warnings and alerts about natural hazards to local Civil Defence Emergency Management (CDEM) Groups, central government authorities, local authorities, emergency services, lifeline utilities and broadcasters. This includes a formal agreement with national broadcast media.

Emergency Mobile Alerts are sent to all mobile phones to warn of emergency events. You don't need to sign up or download an app. The alerts are designed to keep people safe and are broadcast to all capable phones from targeted cell towers. The alerts can be targeted to areas affected by serious hazards and will only be sent when there is a serious threat to life, health or property and, in some cases, for test purposes. Other national alerts are provided by MetService when there are severe weather warnings.

LOCAL ALERTS AND WARNINGS CHANNELS

If you are able to connect to the internet, check your local council's website and social media accounts for updates on the ongoing situation. Also your Civil Defence Emergency Management Group website and social media accounts. National updates will be available on NEMA's website: www.civildefence.govt.nz.

Local Civil Defence Emergency Management Groups are collections of councils and territorial authorities responsible for Civil Defence emergency matters in specific areas. CDEM Groups are responsible for relaying national alerts and warnings to their own communities via local warning systems. They can also initiate alerts about local threats (such as floods).

RADIO

If the power goes out, a solar- or battery-powered radio or your car radio can help you keep up to date with the latest news.

NEMA advises that in times of crisis or Civil Defence emergency, a battery-powered radio, or a car radio, remain essential lifelines if the power is out and other forms of communication are unavailable. Radio New Zealand (RNZ) is New Zealand's statutory Civil Defence lifeline radio broadcaster, providing vital information and updates as they come to hand. RNZ frequencies are shown in the section 'Emergency Information and Contacts' on page 179.

PROMPTS

- Have emergency phone numbers saved in your mobile phone and as a hard copy placed inside a plastic bag in your grab bag. Make copies of important documents (e.g., insurance policy details) as well, scanning documents to keep digitally on your mobile phone as well as hard copies in a plastic bag in your grab bag.
- You can conserve your mobile phone battery by reducing the brightness of the screen and closing the apps you're not using.
- Remember that cell towers depend on electrical power and/or backup batteries and generators to remain functional. Residents in Christchurch initially had mobile phone service in the hours after the major earthquake in 2011; however, as generators ran out of fuel the cell towers went offline.
- Use 'share location' on your mobile phone with members of your household and others and get them to do the same. Know how to find your GPS position on your mobile phone so you can advise someone looking for you. Use Google Maps to provide your precise location and then share this with family and friends.
- Update the voicemail message you may have on your phone, to let friends and family know you're all right.
- Social media can also be used to let your family and friends know that you are safe.

TRANSPORT DURING AN EMERGENCY

During an emergency, personal and public transport may be difficult, if not impossible, to use. Roads may be impassable; restrictions put in place that prohibit movement and fuel supplies may be rationed. At all times, emergency event or not, it pays to always have a good amount of gas in the tank of your car – half a tank at least – or a charged-up battery in the case of an EV.

During a flood, you should never drive through flood-waters. Unfortunately, many drivers have little knowledge of driving through flooded roads and over estimate the ability of their cars to make it. Being caught up in flood-waters in your car can quickly become dangerous. Be very cautious approaching flooded roads. It doesn't take a great depth of water to cause a car to stall. Flood-waters can be deceptive, and the power of flowing water can be life-threatening.

Even shallow water can be risky to drive into if it's flowing faster than 7km/hr. If you stall and your car loses its grip on the road surface, then it's possible it could begin to float and be swept along in the flood-waters. Lose traction and you're likely to lose all control.

Even if your car safely makes it through the flooded road, modern cars are packed full of electronics that can become damaged in flood-waters and may need to be replaced.

Water flooding into the air intakes of an internal combustion engine car (an ICE) can quickly stop the car in its tracks. In the case of an EV, the batteries of both fully electric and hybrid models are highly corrosive, giving the potential for a sudden battery fire — even weeks after the event — if they have been exposed to standing water, salt water especially.

Do not try to charge an EV after it has been retrieved from stalling in a flood. Get it inspected by a qualified technician. Although EV battery fires are uncommon, there is still a risk.

THE BEST ADVICE IS SIMPLY DON'T DRIVE YOUR VEHICLE THROUGH FLOOD-WATERS.

Take care when approaching flooded roads; if you have to drive through flood-waters, drive slowly.

While you should always avoid driving on flooded roads, there could be a time when that's not possible; if for instance, flood-waters have risen around you or a flash flood catches you while you're driving.

When the flood-water is over the bonnet, the engine's air intake system will begin drawing in water, eventually causing the engine to stop. And as modern cars are packed with electrical and electronic systems, contact with water means they may fail, in turn meaning that electric-powered windows will cease working. In approaching an unknown depth of water, wind the windows down before entering. If you suddenly find yourself in deep water, the doors will be difficult, even impossible, to open. With the windows down you have a chance to escape while the water is not too deep.

Research has shown that you've got about 1 minute to save yourself if your car goes into deep water and that you should start trying to escape immediately.

The actions you should take can be remembered by the acronym 'SWOC':

S	SEATBELTS – off
W	WINDOWS – open
O	OUT – immediately
C	CHILDREN – first

The oldest children in the car should get out first so that they can help pull younger children out from the outside.

PROMPTS

- An emergency event may hinder your travel because of damage to roads from seismic or weather events, or the lack of fuel supplies to petrol stations.
- Think twice — do you really need to drive through the flooded road? Can you wait? If you must drive through, it's crucial that you wind down the windows before doing so.
- Whether you are driving an EV or a traditional ICE vehicle, the official advice is the same: if it's flooded, forget it, and instead park your car on high ground and wait for the flood-waters to clear.
- If it's possible, stop, and try to reverse out.
- If you absolutely must drive through flood-water and think that the water is safe to pass through, go slowly to avoid making a bow wave. Moving slowly will also make it less likely that your wheels will lose contact with the road and aquaplane.
- Once through the water, be aware that your brakes will be wet and possibly ineffective. Drive slowly, gently pumping the brakes; this will create heat and help to dry out the brakes and restore full braking capabilities.
- Keep a hammer or combination seatbelt cutter and glass-breaking tool in the glovebox in case of an emergency. Either of these tools could help you break through tempered-glass side windows — don't bother trying to break out through the windscreen; they're usually made of laminated glass and virtually impossible to break, even with a hammer.
- Get your windows down as soon as you can. Electrically operated windows should still be workable for a short time.

AFTERMATH

As emergency services respond to callouts following an emergency event — prioritising those in the greatest need of help — you and your household may be in the position of having to deal with injury, damage and recovery by yourselves — although with the support of your neighbours and local community — for a short time at least. Take it day by day but plan for what might involve weeks. Assume the worst: if you are still able to stay in your home, it may be that you will be without power and water for a period of time. If you're unable to be in your home, you will have to consider your options for alternative accommodation, access to food and water and keeping warm.

GET HELP, GIVE HELP

In the immediate aftermath of an emergency, safety is the primary issue, as are mental and physical wellbeing. It may be chaotic as you deal with the impact of the disaster, but in the middle of the uncertainty you must focus on your health, safety and wellbeing and those of the members of your household.

- Administer first aid and seek medical attention for any injured person. Check for injuries. Do not attempt to move seriously injured persons unless they are in immediate danger of death or further injury. If you must move an unconscious person, first stabilise the neck and back, then call for help.
- In the case of serious injury or health condition, phone 111 for an ambulance.

EMERGENCY FIRST AID

First responders may not be able to get to you immediately. In the meantime, do what you can to alleviate injury – stop bleeding, immobilise broken limbs and provide warmth and comfort to injured persons.

Severe bleeding needs to be staunched immediately. Use gauze pads or any clean material and apply pressure onto the wound. Pack gauze dressings directly into wounds where there is uncontrolled bleeding. Unless you are skilled in first aid, it is not advisable to try to control bleeding using a tourniquet.

If bleeding can be controlled, and help still hasn't arrived, inspect the wound every few hours to check there is no infection: rinse the wound gently with clean water and apply new dressings. If the wound becomes infected, flush it gently with an antiseptic solution.

If there's someone trapped in wreckage or similar who needs immediate help, and there are professional responders at hand, having tools such as a crowbar, axe, shovel, sledgehammer and handsaw will be useful. Don't put your life at risk over trying to salvage things. Remember, people matter not things.

IF YOUR HOME AND ITS CONTENTS ARE DAMAGED

Contact your insurance company as soon as possible regarding filing a claim. If you rent your property, contact your landlord and your contents insurance company. Take photos of any damage before you begin the clean-up, it will help speed up the assessment process of your claims. Save photos to the internet in case your mobile phone is lost or damaged. Save all your receipts for post-damage repair and clean-up.

KEEP INFORMED

If your home has lost power, use a solar- or battery-powered radio (or your car radio) to stay up to date with the news on the emergency event. If you still have cell phone service, text or use social media to contact and advise friends and family instead of calling. Phone lines need to be kept clear for emergency calls.

THE MORE THAT HOUSEHOLDS CAN PREPARE WELL FOR SURVIVING AND RECOVERING FROM EMERGENCY EVENTS, THE MORE THAT EMERGENCY SERVICES CAN FOCUS THEIR LIMITED RESOURCES ON THOSE WHO NEED HELP THE MOST.

SAFETY ISSUES WHEN RETURNING TO YOUR HOME

If you are returning home following an emergency, know that it can be both physically and mentally challenging. And above all else, use caution. You may be anxious to see your property but don't go back until local officials say it is safe to return:

- Be aware of possible new safety issues created by the emergency event. Watch for washed-out roads, contaminated buildings, contaminated water, gas leaks, broken glass, damaged electrical wiring and slippery floors.
- Walk carefully around the outside of your property and check for loose power lines, gas leaks and structural damage. If you have any doubts about safety, have your residence inspected by a qualified building inspector or structural engineer before entering.
- Don't go into your damaged home if you smell gas, if flood-waters remain around the building or if the authorities have not declared it safe to enter.
- Keep a solar- or battery-powered radio with you for emergency updates.
- If you can't return to your home, you will need to think about temporary alternative accommodation — with extended family or friends, or in a local community shelter, local motel or marae.
- If you're renting, let your landlord or housing agency know as soon as possible that you are unable to return to the property.
- When you can and if it's safe, take photos and videos of damage to provide evidence for insurance claims. Also note down the actions you have taken to make your property safe and secure. Keep receipts for any expenses relating to repairs.

SECURE YOUR HOME

Secure your home as soon as possible. Emergency repairs to stop rain and wind getting in can be done with sheets of plywood, tarpaulins and plastic sheets fixed over broken windows with boards or gaffer tape. Use tarpaulins or plastic sheeting over holes in the roof. Make your property safe and secure as much as you can.

If your house is uninhabitable and you are living elsewhere, board-up doors and windows and any holes in fences to discourage trespassers. Most people are decent and are more likely to offer help. However, while looting in New Zealand is rare, it can happen. Especially during times of major disasters when opportunism comes to the fore and/ or some people may be under increased strain because of the event.

In a quote often attributed to Vladimir Lenin, the founder and first head of Soviet Russia, it's said, 'Every society is 3 meals away from revolution.' American writer Alfred Henry Lewis put it at '9 meals between mankind and anarchy'. A well secured house is less enticing.

EMERGENCY REPAIRS

You may want to quickly get into emergency repairs following an emergency event, but it will pay to first give some initial thought to what you are able to do, and what is best done by professionals. It is recommended that you contact your insurance company first in either case. If you need to do urgent work to make your home clean and safe, make a record of the work you do. Take before-and-after photos. Keep copies of the bills you pay.

In the case of dealing with storm damage, the following are a few dos and don'ts according to experts who assisted in the aftermath of Cyclone Gabrielle in 2023:

Damaged roofs – The real problem when it comes to damaged roofs is not pieces flying off (although these present a real danger and a good reason not to venture outside while a storm is still raging), but water getting into the ceiling. If it looks like roof tiles or irons have come off, the first thing to do is look up into the crawl space and identify whether water is getting in. If there's water, you should drill a hole in the ceiling and put some buckets underneath to prevent the ceiling from collapsing. It's not advisable to go out in high winds on a ladder to fix anything else. Contact emergency services or professional roofers.
– Michael Quellin, Auckland Roofing Solutions

Fallen trees – Homeowners shouldn't try to attempt clearing a fallen tree on their own, especially if it has downed power lines. Fallen trees are incredibly dangerous. If it's fallen on a house, the wood could be under tension, so if you take a chain saw to it, it could snap at any time or kick back the saw and cause injury. Only people who are experienced with a chain saw should attempt it and should start by cutting away small segments. However, it may be safer to wait for an arborist to look at the tree and in the meantime put up a tarpaulin or an old duvet where the tree has damaged a house.
– Mike Jarvis, The Treeman

Broken windows – If a window requires ladder access it might not be repairable until after the storm has passed. Holding a glass pane in the wind is like holding a sail, and the last thing you want is to be climbing a ladder with one. Instead, get a strong plastic bag and gaffer tape and tape up 2 layers, inside and outside the window, to stop rain from getting in. If there is loose glass, this can be knocked out with a broom, but in general glass shards stuck in a window should not be touched.
– Nick Abercrombie, United Glass

Flooded homes – If flood-waters are rising, the priority is to move people and precious possessions, such as photo albums, out of the reach of flood-waters. Many people will want to take to flooded areas after waters have receded with buckets, but they should only attempt this if they have protective gear such as gloves, masks and goggles on. Best to leave it to the professionals who will extract standing water with industrial-grade extractor machines. In the meantime, householders could clean up any debris that might obstruct tradespeople, again with personal protective equipment. This will definitely help speed up the job.
– Fred Morley, Chem-Dry

SAFETY WITH YOUR GAS AND ELECTRICAL SUPPLY

Underground gas pipes and cables, as well as overhead power lines and other electricity and gas equipment, run under and over and around properties, and it's easy to become complacent around them and their operation and potential for danger in the aftermath of an emergency event.

Gas smells a bit like rotten eggs. If you think you smell gas, it's important that you leave the immediate area and contact your gas supplier as there may be a leak. Gas is highly flammable, which means if there's a leak combined with the likes of a spark from lighting a candle, flicking a light switch or using a mobile phone, it could ignite and lead to an explosion or fire. Therefore, before contacting your gas supplier, you should leave the immediate area and not use any electrical devices, light switches, matches or mobile phones in the vicinity of the leaking gas.

If you smell gas inside your house:

- Turn off all gas appliances.
- Don't smoke (including e-cigarettes), and extinguish any naked flames.
- Don't use any electrical equipment, switches, mobile phones or electronic equipment.
- Vacate the building.
- Contact your gas supplier.

If you smell gas outside your house:

- Move away from the area, upwind of the source.
- Don't smoke (including e-cigarettes), and extinguish any naked flames.
- Close windows and doors to stop gas entering buildings.
- Turn off any machinery that may be running if you can.
- Advise your gas supplier.

ELECTRICITY

Outages can be checked on your power supplier's website and sometimes it's possible to get an estimate of when power will be restored. You can also report outages that haven't been identified yet. Listen to your battery-powered radio or check your mobile phone for updates.

- Pillar boxes – If you're connected to the electricity network by underground cable rather than overhead line, you'll have a pillar box on your boundary or roadside. If your pillar box is damaged or in a location where it could be damaged (by a car for instance), contact your electricity distributor for an assessment. Never touch the pillar box.
- Earth pegs – Your earth peg is an important part of your building's electrical safety system. It ensures that any electrical faults inside the building go into the ground, keeping the people inside safe from serious shocks. Earth pegs are usually near your electricity meter. If your earth peg is damaged or worn, contact an electrician to ensure it's safe. Never touch the earth peg.

SAFETY WITH YOUR WATER SUPPLY

Teaching everyone in the household how to turn off the water is important. Unlike gas, water can be turned on and off with no safety concerns.

Water lines into the house could leak or burst following an emergency event or could be polluted from cracked main water pipes. Following a major event that could have caused pipe breakages it's a good idea to turn off the water until you hear from authorities that the water supply is safe.

Locate the shut-off valve (known as a toby), which is usually inside a box on the perimeter of your property where the water supply enters your property; for most residential houses this will most likely be on the front boundary. Make sure that the valve can be completely shut off, turning it clockwise. Check that your toby is not jammed open and that it closes fully. If it is stuck or only partially closes, fix those problems and ensure it shuts off completely.

INSURANCE

If you don't have insurance, it can take more time to get back on your feet, although support is available to help you cope through what's happened.

Your private home insurance policy includes an amount for natural emergency insurance, provided by the Natural Hazards Commission (NHC). NHC provides insured homeowners with natural hazards cover to help rebuild or repair their homes and limited areas of land if they are damaged by a natural hazard event.

You have natural hazards cover if you have a home insurance policy that includes fire insurance (and most do). The premium you pay your insurer includes a Natural Hazards Insurance levy (NHI levy), which gives you access to hazards insurance. It's important to understand what is and isn't covered by NHI and by your insurer.

NHI cover insures you against loss or damage from:

- Earthquakes.
- Natural landslip.
- Volcanic eruption.
- Hydrothermal activity.
- Tsunami.

It insures your residential land (within limits) against storm and flood damage. It also insures you against fire resulting from any of these natural emergencies. If your home isn't damaged during an emergency event but damage is imminent as a direct result of one, cover may also apply.

The Insurance Council of New Zealand recommends that insurance claims are made online rather than over the phone. Photograph damage to your property and contents. Mark on the outside and inside walls of your home the highest points of flooding and take a photograph of these. Also photograph any insured items that you may have removed from the property.

MENTAL WELLBEING

Experiencing a disaster can be overwhelming. It's normal if you and your household feel upset and physically drained during and after an emergency event. Your mental and emotional wellbeing is important. If you feel you're not coping, talk to a health professional. Seek medical help from your doctor or a mental health provider familiar with the effects of disasters.

Some people may not have a reaction. Others may have delayed reactions that show up days, weeks or even months after the event. Not everyone has reactions right away or reacts the same. Your symptoms may go and then come back again when something makes you think of the disaster.

After a disaster, be sure to talk to someone about how you are feeling. There may be a specialist post-disaster crisis counsellor appointed in your area. People can also connect with like-minded groups for support. Rural Support Trust can offer assistance to rural people and farms as they are specialised in this field and understand the stressors of rural life.

Sources of help include:

- 1737 is a free service, enabling you to talk with a counsellor – free call or free text any time, 24 hours a day.
- Lifeline – 0800 543 354 (0800 LIFELINE) or free text 4357 (HELP).
- Youthline – 0800 376 633, free text 234 or email talk@youthline.co.nz or their online chat (available on their website).
- Ministry of Health – Contact for advice on understanding emotional reactions to emergencies and positive ways of coping.

The aftermath of the devasting flooding in the Eskdale Valley, Hawke's Bay, following Cyclone Gabrielle in 2023. A flash flood sweeping through the Esk Valley saw the Esk River overrun its banks, submerging properties and burying some homes in silt up to their roof lines. Damage was widespread across Hawke's Bay with flood-waters damaging and washing away bridges, closing and collapsing roads and bringing down slips. Numerous settlements in the area were cut off and many people required evacuation.

PROMPTS

- Continue to follow advice from local authorities, emergency services and your local Civil Defence Emergency Management Group.
- Be on the alert for new problems that may be caused by more rainfall and landslides, new flooding or earthquake aftershocks.
- When it's safe to do so, check in on neighbours and others who also may need help.
- Turn off the mains water supply and mains electricity supply at source if there are breaks in the water or sewer lines, or in the electricity supply. Take care when checking and keep people away from power lines that have come down.
- Report gas leaks immediately to your gas supplier. Don't turn off gas unless instructed to by your supplier.
- Check house foundations and roof for cracks and damage.
- Avoid using your car unless necessary: during the emergency event and in the aftermath of it, streets need to be kept as clear as possible for emergency vehicles. If you do drive somewhere, keep a lookout for downed power lines, landslides and flooded roads.
- For insurance claims purposes, take photographs of any damage to either your house and/or its contents.
- A power outage over many hours or longer may mean that food in your fridge and freezer will not be safe to eat. Do not re-freeze food that has completely thawed. Food that has been in flood-waters – with the exception of canned food – must be thrown out. Wash canned food with clean water before opening.

- If there was a water outage, when the supply is restored, run the cold tap for a few minutes to get rid of any sediment and other debris that may have got into the pipes. If you're unsure about the look or smell of the water coming out of your taps, report this to your water supplier. In the meantime, boil water for 1–2 minutes before drinking until the problem is resolved.

EMERGENCY INFORMATION AND CONTACTS

Before, during and after an emergency event there are many sources of information and emergency services you can call on for help and advice.

WHO IS CIVIL DEFENCE? HOW DOES THE EMERGENCY RESPONSE WORK?

'Civil Defence' is not 1 organisation, it's a big co-operative effort made up of lots of agencies. In an emergency response, all the agencies work together to provide support to communities in need. These agencies include local councils, NZ Police, Fire and Emergency (FENZ), Health NZ, Waka Kotahi, MSD, MBIE, Red Cross, to name just a few.

There are 16 Civil Defence Emergency Management Groups across the country. During non-emergency times, it's these groups and their regional Emergency

Management Office's role to coordinate emergency planning with all these agencies who have responsibilities during an emergency.

These responsibilities include things like firefighting, fixing broken infrastructure, search and rescue, providing emergency financial support systems, caring for animals, providing council services and giving public health advice.

The National Emergency Management Agency's (NEMA) role during an emergency is to provide support to regional groups during an emergency, coordinate requests for assistance and provide the government's response to a national emergency.

During an emergency response that is led by CDEMs (i.e., in the case of earthquakes, floods, volcanic eruptions, storms and tsunamis), local councils lead and coordinate the response with all the partner agencies from their Emergency Operations Centres. However, councils and emergency management office staff can't do all of this alone. Emergencies need everyone — including individuals, whānau and communities to share the responsibility of helping each other when things are broken.

So, during an emergency, if you've seen a local council staff member, police officer, fire fighter, contractor or a response team member involved in the response, then you've seen 'Civil Defence'.

WHEN IT HAPPENS

NEMA supports regional Civil Defence Emergency Management Groups during a disaster. It manages the central government's response and recovery functions for national emergencies, and supports the management of local and regional emergencies, providing on-the-ground emergency management and co-ordination to help people get through natural or man-made emergencies.

Emergency response is coordinated by local and regional councils.

There is a coordinated effort to assist people facing emergencies between Fire and Emergency New Zealand (FENZ), Police, Ambulance, Civil Defence, the Red Cross and other community agencies, depending on the situation.

View the NEMA website and/or contact their office to find out information on local hazards and community response arrangements. For details about who to contact in your area, visit NEMA's 'Get Ready' website. Contact your local Civil Defence Emergency Management Group to see if there is a community response plan for your area.

EMERGENCY SERVICES

New Zealand has 3 main emergency services: Fire and Emergency, Police, and Ambulance.

If you or anyone else is in immediate danger or your property is at risk, call emergency services on 111. Calling 111 is free. You can call this number from a mobile phone, even if you have no credit available.

If you have hearing or speech difficulties, you can register for the New Zealand Police 111 TXT service so you can text Police, Fire or Ambulance in an emergency. Refer to the NZ Police website for more information.

Links to information useful ahead of, during, and after an emergency include:

- Civil Defence Emergency Management (CDEM) Group – www.civildefence.govt.nz
- Earthquake insurance – www.naturalhazards.govt.nz
- Earthquake monitoring and reporting – www.geonet.org.nz
- Food safety in an emergency – www.mpi.govt.nz/funding-rural-support/adverse-events/food-safety-in-natural-disasters-and-emergencies
- Get Ready – getready.govt.nz
- National Emergency Management Agency (NEMA) – www.civildefence.govt.nz
- State Highway conditions – www.journeys.nzta.govt.nz
- Weather warnings and forecasts – www.metservice.com

Regularly listen to the radio and TV for the latest news and any alerts or instructions. Visit the NEMA Civil Defence website for updates on current emergencies. Check in with your local and regional councils for information on your local Civil Defence Emergency Management Group. It's important you also follow the directions of Police or other emergency services. If you are asked to evacuate, make sure you're able to get out quickly.

EMERGENCY MOBILE ALERTS

Emergency Mobile Alerts are alerts that can be sent to your mobile phone, without needing to sign up or download an app. Most mobile phones can receive these alerts.

NEMA, Civil Defence Emergency Management Groups and other responsible agencies will only send Emergency Mobile Alerts when there is a threat to life or significant disruption.

When you receive an emergency alert, follow the advice and make sure you are safe. Then make sure your friends and family are safe by sharing the information on social media or by text (if you can). The National Emergency Management Agency (NEMA) is responsible for the national warning system for tsunami alerts. This includes a formal agreement with national broadcast media.

Other national alerts are provided by MetService when there are severe weather warnings.

SOME GENERAL SUPPORT SERVICES

- Citizens Advice Bureau – www.cab.org.nz
- Community Emergency Hubs (in some parts of the country)
- The Ministry of Health – www.health.govt.nz
- All Right – www.allright.org.nz
- KidsHealth NZ has a page dedicated to helping kids cope with a natural disaster – www.kidshealth.org.nz
- Mental Health Foundation of New Zealand – www.mentalhealth.org.nz/
- Work and Income – www.workandincome.govt.nz

RADIO

The National Emergency Management Agency (NEMA) advises that in times of crisis or Civil Defence emergency a battery-powered radio, or a car radio, remain essential lifelines if power is out, and other forms of communication are unavailable. Radio New Zealand (RNZ) is New Zealand's statutory Civil Defence lifeline radio broadcaster, providing vital information and updates as they come to hand.

In an emergency, tune in to RNZ on its frequencies below. Frequencies are updated from time to time and an up-to-date list of frequencies will be available at www.rnz.co.nz/listen/amfm.

RNZ FREQUENCIES

(* = Community operated transmitters)

NORTH ISLAND	FREQUENCIES
Kaitaia	National AM 837 National FM 101.1 Concert 100.3
Russell/Kororāreka	Concert 97.3
Kaikohe	National AM 981 National FM 101.5 Concert 98.3
Whangārei	National AM 837 National FM 104.4 National – Lower Northland 101.2 Concert 100.4 Concert – Lower Northland 105.2
Auckland/Tāmaki Makaurau	National AM 756 National FM 101.4 Concert 92.6 AM Network (Parliament) 882
Hamilton/Kirikiriroa	National AM 1143 National FM 101.0 Concert 91.4 AM Network (Parliament) 1494
Tauranga	National AM 819 National FM 101.4 Concert 91.4 AM Network (Parliament) 657
Whakatāne	National FM 101.7 Concert 95.3
Tokoroa	National AM 729 National FM 101.0
Rotorua	National AM 1188 National FM 101.5 Concert 90.3
Te Kūiti*	National FM 94.0

NORTH ISLAND	FREQUENCIES
Taupō	National FM 101.6 National FM Acacia Bay 104.8 Concert 97.3
Gisborne/Tairāwhiti	National AM 1314 National FM 101.3 Concert 97.3
Napier/Ahuriri	National AM 630 National FM 101.5 Concert 91.1 AM Network (Parliament) 909
New Plymouth/ Ngāmotu	National FM 101.2 Concert 91.6
Whanganui	National AM 567 National FM 101.6 Concert 99.2
Palmerston North	National AM 1449 National FM 101.0 Concert 89.0
Masterton/ Whakaoriori	National AM 1071 National FM 101.5 Concert 99.1
Kāpiti	National AM 567 National FM 101.5 Concert 98.3
Wellington/ Te Whanganui-a-Tara	National AM 567 National FM 101.3 National FM – Hutt Valley/Eastern Bays 96.1 Concert 92.5 Concert – Hutt Valley/Eastern Bays 96.1 AM Network (Parliament) 657

SOUTH ISLAND	FREQUENCIES
Nelson/Whakatū	National AM 1116 National FM 101.6 Concert 91.2
Tākaka/Golden Bay/ Mohua*	National FM 98.2
Blenheim	National AM 567 National FM 101.7 Concert 99.3

SOUTH ISLAND	FREQUENCIES
Westport/Kawatiri	National AM 1458 Concert 98.9
Greymouth/ Māwhera	National FM 101.1 Concert 95.5
Christchurch/ Ōtautahi	National AM 657 National FM 101.7 Concert 89.7 Concert – Akaroa 95.1 Concert – Sumner 99.7 AM Network (Parliament) 963
Ōmarama*	National FM 97.3
Ashburton/ Hakatere	National FM 101.3
Lake Tekapo/Tekapō*	National FM 93.4
Otematata*	National FM 106.7
Timaru	National AM 918 National FM 101.1 Concert 99.5
Wānaka	National FM 101.0 Concert 95.4
Queenstown/Tāhuna	National FM 101.6 Concert 98.4
Alexandra	National FM 101.5 Concert 97.5
Te Anau*	National FM 101.6
Milford Sound/ Piopiotahi*	National FM 92.0
Dunedin/Ōtepoti	National AM 810 National FM 101.4 Concert 92.6 or 99.0 Concert – Mosgiel 99.4 AM Network (Parliament) 900
Invercargill/ Waihōpai	National AM 720 National FM 101.2 Concert 90.0 AM Network (Parliament) 1314

Today's world can, at times, feel increasingly uncertain and continually disrupted by crises such as pandemics, extreme weather events driven by climate change and infrastructure failure. At the same time there's also a growing awareness of the dangers posed by our massive digital interconnectedness: almost every part of our lives is run by computers linked to the internet. Our electronic control systems — the systems that bring water to our taps, electricity to our homes and businesses, groceries to our supermarkets, petrol to our local petrol stations — have become highly vulnerable to disruption by human error and by hacking.

The size of recent emergency events has shown us that official responder agencies can only do so much when these events happen and may be quickly overwhelmed. As individuals and communities, we need to do our bit as well — to look after ourselves, our families and our neighbours, to not only mitigate and survive the effects of such events on our lives but also allow responder agencies to prioritise help for those who need it most. It's about simple steps such as putting together a store of foodstuffs and water that can carry you through a week or 2; making plans for our households when it comes to evacuation and communications. Ensuring we have alternatives for cooking, lighting, warmth and recharging devices. To learn about resilience and recovery. To be prepared.

ACKNOWLEDGEMENTS AND CREDITS

ACKNOWLEDGEMENTS

The author would like to acknowledge and thank the following for their assistance, information, and for approval to use material in this book. Special thanks go to the National Emergency Management Agency (NEMA) and the Wellington Region Emergency Management Office (WREMO).

Clive Matthew-Wilson (safe driving in flood-waters)
Environment Texas and Luke Metzger (powering your house using your electric car)
FEMA (Federal Emergency Management Agency) (various information throughout)
Fire and Emergency NZ (wildfires)
Fred Morley Chem-Dry (New Zealand) Ltd (quoted in 'Cyclone Gabrielle: Who to call, what to do if the roof comes off or windows smash': 14 February 2023 Stuff Ltd / Jonathan Killick)
Genesis Energy (powering your house using your electric car)
GNS Science (the Institute of Geological and Nuclear Sciences Limited) re seismic activity warnings: Reference entry: GNS Science (n.d.). *Ash.* GNS Science. www.gns.cri.nz/our-science/natural-hazards-and-risks/volcanoes/ash/)
Jonathan Beaver (powering your house using your electric car)
MetService (Severe Weather Outlooks, Watches and Warnings)
Michael Quellin of Auckland Roofing Solutions (quoted in 'Cyclone Gabrielle: Who to call, what to do if the roof comes off or windows smash': 14 February 2023 Stuff Ltd / Jonathan Killick)
Mike Jarvis of The Treeman (quoted in 'Cyclone Gabrielle: Who to call, what to do if the roof comes off or windows smash': 14 February 2023 Stuff Ltd / Jonathan Killick)

National Roads and Motorists' Association Ltd (safe driving in flood-waters)
Natural Hazards Commission (hazards insurance / 'Climate Change and Insurance' by Tina Mitchell)
Neil Duncan
NEMA (National Emergency Management Agency) (information from the Get Ready! website and other information throughout)
Nick Abercrombie of United Glass (quoted in 'Cyclone Gabrielle: Who to call, what to do if the roof comes off or windows smash': 14 February 2023 Stuff Ltd / Jonathan Killick)
NOAA (National Oceanic and Atmospheric Administration) National Weather Service (tsunami and space weather)
Office of Emergency Management, Seattle Govt (cyber attack and infrastructure failure)
Office of the Ombudsman (*Insights and observations: The Chief Ombudsman's report on extreme weather events 2023.* Copyright © Office of the Ombudsman 2023. All rights reserved. This work is licensed under the Creative Commons Attribution 4.0 International License. To view a copy of this license, visit https:// creativecommons.org)
Powerco (gas and electricity safety information on website July 2024)
Radio New Zealand
Stuff Limited ('Cyclone Gabrielle: Who to call, what to do if the roof comes off or windows smash': 14 February 2023 Stuff Ltd / Jonathan Killick)
The Provident Prepper (alternatives to toilet paper)
Watercare Services Ltd
Wikipedia (extract from list of natural disasters in New Zealand https://en.wikipedia.org/wiki/List_of_natural_disasters_in_New_Zealand
WREMO (Wellington Region Emergency Management Office) (various information throughout and the two-bucket toilet system: Massey University led a collaboration with Wellington Water, Regional Public Health, WREMO and the councils to understand the process of capture, containment, emptying and transport, treatment and disposal or re-use of excreta, if using the two-bucket system. This led to the councils, WREMO, Wellington Water and Te Whatu Ora/Regional Public Health conducting a project including a wider range of stakeholders to plan for emergency sanitation. Stakeholders were from Ngāti Toa, the disability sector and managers and contractors of solid waste.
'Every society is three meals away from chaos': **Vladimir Lenin**, the founder and first head of Soviet Russia.
'Those of us who are well fed, well garmented and well ordered, ought not to forget that necessity makes frequently the root of crime. It is well for us to recollect that even in our own law-abiding, not to say virtuous cases, the only barrier between us and anarchy is the last nine meals we've had.': **Alfred Henry Lewis**, American investigative journalist, lawyer, novelist, editor, and writer (*New York Journal*, October 13, 1896.

PHOTO AND ILLUSTRATION CREDITS

Alyse Hedley – pp28, 108, 171
Fire and Emergency NZ – p57
GNS – pp5 (Margaret Low), 14 (Steven Sherburn), 20 (Margaret Low), 27 (Margaret Low), 51 (Lloyd Homer)
NASA – p9 (a composite satellite image of Cyclone Gabrielle, taken February 13. Source: NASA/EOSDIS Worldview)
NEMA – pp22, 23, 46, 64, 97, 104
NIWA – pp6, 33, 37, 157, 160
WREMO – pp117, 140

READING

How to Survive a Crisis — Lessons in Resilience and Avoiding Disaster, David Ormond, Viking 2023

INDEX

111
- 111 phone calls 148, 153, 161, 176
- Police 111 TXT service 177

A

aftermath 160–72
- prompts 172–73
- *see also under* specific emergencies, e.g. earthquakes – what to do after an earthquake

aftershocks 26, 76
alerts
- Emergency Mobile Alerts 81, 153
- local alerts and warning channels 154

Ambulance 176
ash fall from volcanic eruptions 53–54, 55–56
- emergency supplies 55

auroras 63

B

batteries 40, 67, 73, 82, 86, 96, 101, 102, 125, 132, 152
- electric vehicle and car batteries 127–30, 157
- hearing-aid batteries 98
- radio batteries 82, 100, 152

bleeding 80, 105, 161
bone breaks 80, 105
burns 80, 105

C

Canterbury earthquakes, 2010 and 2011 8, 27, 134, 155
car emergency supply kit 98–99
carbon monoxide 110, 115, 125
cardiopulmonary resuscitation (CPR) 68, 81, 105–06
Carrington Event, 1859 63
cash on hand 83, 86, 90, 124
civil defence 174–76
Civil Defence Centres (CDCs) 69–70
Civil Defence Emergency Management (CDEM) Groups 29, 31, 39, 42, 47, 48, 49, 55, 63, 69, 70, 82, 153, 154, 172, 174–76, 177
climate change 11–12, 19
communications in emergencies 147–49, 155; *see also* household communications plan; information sources; phones; radio

Community Emergency Hubs 70, 91, 178
community preparedness 70
contamination
 flood-water 30
 from volcanic ash 54, 56
counselling 171
covering your body, head and neck 24
Covid-19 pandemic 8, 61
cyber-attacks 61–62
Cyclone Gabrielle 9–10, 18, 41, 128, 129, 147, 165
Cyclone Hale 9
cyclones *see* tropical cyclones

D

dangerous items
 chemical and biohazard contamination 31
 move higher to avoid flood 30
debris flows 33–34, 35
Department of Conservation 55
disabilities and emergencies 25, 26, 69, 91, 135, 141, 148, 151
document storage and copies 80, 90
driving and cars 82, 172
 after a landslide 35
 car emergency supply kit 98–99
 driving through flood-water 30, 44, 68, 74–75, 83, 156–58, 159
 Drop, Cover and Hold 24
 State Highway conditions 177
 when a tornado funnel is nearby 38
 when caught in a lightning storm 43
 when there are volcanic hazards 55
 when there's warning of a possible tsunami 49
 during a wildfire 57, 59
Drop, Cover and Hold 22–25, 26, 49, 74
 if you have a mobility impairment or use a cane 25
 if you use a walker or wheelchair 25
 if you're driving 24
 if you're in an elevator 24
 if you're in bed 25
 if you're near the coast 25
 if you're outside 24
dust masks 96

E

earthquakes 16, 17, 20–21, 74
 caused by volcanic activity 54
 contacts 177
 long and strong in a tsunami zone 48, 49, 50, 75
 what to do after an earthquake 26
 what to do before an earthquake 21
 what to do during an earthquake 22–25
 see also Canterbury earthquakes, 2010 and 2011
elderly people 26, 69, 113
electric vehicles (EVs) 82, 156, 157, 159
 used as power stations 127–30
electricity
 backup/replacement power and accessories 124–25
 broken power lines 35–36, 40, 45, 68
 items that may conduct electricity during a storm 40, 42, 44
 outages 7, 86, 160, 167–68, 172
 power surges 40, 42, 79, 126, 132
 safety 167–68

    shut-off and safety 26, 29, 40, 42, 63, 68, 79, 90, 108, 109, 113, 125, 132–33
    during a space weather event 63
    uninterruptible power supply (UPS) 91, 148
elevators
    do not use in an emergency 26
    Drop, Cover and Hold 24
email 149
Emergency Assistance Centres (EACs) 69–70
Emergency Mobile Alerts 81, 153, 177–78
emergency services 11, 16, 66, 82, 176–78
    general support services 178
emergency supplies
    prompts 101–02
    see also car emergency supply kit; grab bags; household emergency supply kit; workplace emergency supply kit
eruptions *see* volcanic activity
escape routes 88
evacuation 29, 35, 47–48, 49, 50, 57–58, 67–68, 76–77, 85, 108–09, 114
evacuation plan 86–88
extreme weather events 8, 11, 17, 18
2023 8–11, 18, 128

F

families 26, 44
Fire and Emergency New Zealand (FENZ) 174, 176
fires
    following earthquakes 26
    see also wildfires
first aid 26, 42, 68, 103
    contents for first aid kit 103–05
    emergency first aid 80–81, 103–05, 161–62
    prompts 106
flashlights and torches 31, 40, 67, 73, 82, 86, 96, 99, 101, 102, 125, 132
    waterproof flashlight 29, 31
flooding 17, 18, 28, 41, 44–45, 74, 109
    Auckland Anniversary Weekend, 2023 9, 10
    cleaning and drying your home 32, 166
    what to do after a flood 31–32, 163
    what to do before a flood 29–30
    what to do during a flood 30–31
    see also Cyclone Gabrielle; Cyclone Hale; tsunamis
food supply 7, 13, 16, 83, 85, 86, 94, 95–96, 98, 99, 111–12
    emergency food considerations 113–14
    meal preparation 115–16
    prompts 122–23
    safety and sanitation 31, 114, 172, 177
    storing food 112–13

G

gas appliances 86, 99, 102, 115, 125
gas supply 26, 32, 67, 73, 112, 124
    safety 163, 166–67, 172
    shut-off 27, 29, 78, 84, 89, 93, 108, 119, 124, 130, 155
generators 110, 125–27, 128–29, 148
'Get Ready' website 176, 177
grab bags 16, 29, 39, 57, 67, 68, 73, 80, 90, 99–100
    basic supplies and optional extras 100–01
    checklist 92
Great East Japan Earthquake, 2011 47

H

hand washing 142–43
health crises 17, 18; *see also* Covid-19 pandemic
help, getting and giving 161–62
household communications plan 82, 88–89, 149–51
- emergency meeting places 73, 86–87, 151
- preparing for and during an emergency 152–54

household emergency plan 16, 73, 84, 85–93
- can't get home 85
- prompts 93
- stuck at home 85, 107, 160

household emergency supply kits 16, 55, 67, 73, 88, 95
- prompts 101–02
- recommended items 95–98, 110

hypothermia 81, 105

I

infants 26, 97, 113
information sources 29, 31, 34, 35, 39, 41–42, 48, 49, 55, 66–67, 81–82, 162, 174–82
- contact details 177

infrastructure failure 62
insurance 70–71, 77, 90, 164, 169–70
Insurance Council of New Zealand 170
internet 7, 86, 147, 149, 182

L

lahars (volcanic mudflows) 53, 54
land deformation from volcanic activity 54
landslides 17, 33–34, 75
- what to do after a landslide 35–36
- what to do before a landslide 34
- what to do during a landslide 35

lava flows 54
lightning 37, 39, 40, 42, 43–44, 53
looting 164

M

masks 55, 56, 58, 96, 166
meeting places 73, 86–87, 151
mental wellbeing 170–71, 178
MetService 29, 31, 35, 39, 41–42, 67, 177, 178

N

National Emergency Management Agency (NEMA) 16, 48, 67, 153, 175–76, 177, 178
National Health Insurance (NHI) levy 169
natural disasters 15, 19
- New Zealand's worst emergencies since mid 1800s 17–18
- *see also* earthquakes; flooding; landslides; storms; tsunamis; volcanic activity

natural hazards insurance 71, 169
neighbours 30, 35, 42, 44, 69, 70, 83, 94, 106

P

pandemics 61
pets 29, 35, 49, 56, 91, 117
phones 26, 67, 73, 78, 82, 89, 97, 98, 100, 102, 149, 152–53, 155, 162
- 111 calls 148, 153, 161, 176
- Emergency Mobile Alerts 81, 153–54, 177–78
- no phone service 7, 10, 72, 86, 87, 147–48, 155
- phone numbers 73, 85, 86, 153, 155

tracking household members via mobile phones 81, 153
using to access information 68, 168
using to photograph documents 80, 90, 155
using to video home contents and externals 21
photos of damage 27, 36, 90, 162, 163, 164, 170
planning 39, 72–73, 84–94
Police 174, 175, 176, 177
111 TXT service 177
power line falls 35–36, 40, 45, 68, 133
power packs 82, 132, 152
power stations 110, 126
electric vehicles used as power stations 127–30
preparedness 65–67
community preparedness 70
four most important aspects 16
a quick guide to preparedness and action 72–83
property damage 26, 27, 27, 50, 162, 163, 164
emergency repairs 164–66

R

radio
emergency information broadcasts 26, 29, 30, 41, 42, 48, 49, 67, 68, 81, 82, 86, 93, 149, 154, 162, 163, 168, 177
RNZ frequencies 82, 179–81
solar or battery-powered radios 12, 40, 68, 82, 86, 96, 100, 125, 152, 154, 162, 163, 168
Radio New Zealand (RNZ) 154, 178–81
Red Cross 66, 68, 103, 105, 174, 176
returning home following an emergency 163
roof damage 165
Rural Support Trust 171

S

secure your home 164
septic tanks 143
severe weather outlooks, watches and warnings 41–42
shelter 24, 69, 73, 74, 76–77, 85, 88, 107
emergency shelter 38, 43, 44, 77, 84, 109–10, 163
prompts 110
staying in place 58, 85, 107–08, 160
snowstorms 43
social media 26, 89, 149, 154, 155, 162
solar flares 63
solar-powered lights 132
solar-powered phone charger 152
space blanket (Mylar blanket) 43
space weather 62–63
special assistance 26
special needs and emergencies 26, 69, 91
St John 68, 103, 106
storm water drainage 34
storms 17, 37–38, 75
what to do after a severe storm 44–45
what to do before a severe storm 39–42, 133
what to do during a severe storm 42–44, 133
see also extreme weather events; lightning; thunderstorms; tornadoes; tropical cyclones

T

Tangiwai disaster, 1953 52
Tarawera eruption, 1886 52
Taupō eruption, ca. AD 232 52
television (TV) 40, 41, 48, 67, 68, 79, 81, 132, 177
text messaging 26, 89, 149, 162
thunderstorms 37, 38, 39, 42; *see also* lightning
toilet paper alternatives 144–45
toilets in emergencies 79, 96, 134–37
  for apartment dwellers 142
  chemical toilets and portaloos 143
  disposing of urine and faeces 139, 140–41, 142
  how to build a long drop 137–38
  how to build an emergency bucket toilet 138–41
  if someone is sick 146
  prompts 145–46
  for those with accessibility needs or limited mobility 141
torches *see* flashlights and torches
tornadoes 38, 39, 69
transport during an emergency 26, 156–59; *see also* driving and cars
trees
  fallen trees 165
  trees near power lines 40, 133, 165
tropical cyclones 38; *see also* Cyclone Gabrielle; Cyclone Hale
tsunamis 25, 26, 46–47, 75–76, 81, 178
  evacuation zone 85
  what to do after a tsunami 49–50
  what to do before a tsunami 47–48
  what to do during a tsunami or when a warning has been issued 49

U

uninterruptible power supply (UPS) 91, 148
USB light sticks 132
utilities 124–25
  broken utility lines 35–36
  shut-off and safety 77, 89–90, 124

V

valuable items 30
volcanic activity 17, 18, 51–53, 76
  consequent hazards 53–55
  emergency supplies to deal with ash fall 55
  places most at risk of ash fall 55
  what to do after volcanic activity 56
  what to do during volcanic activity 55–56
  see also Tarawera eruption, 1886; Taupō eruption, ca. AD 232; Whakaari/White Island eruption, 2019
volcanic gas emissions 54

W

walker users 13
wastewater 135, 143
water supply 13, 16, 42, 82, 85, 86, 94, 95–96, 98, 99, 107, 110, 111–12, 113, 160
  contamination and treatment 31, 54, 56, 120–21
  emergency sources of water 86, 119–20
  preparing containers of water 118–19

prompts 122–23
safety 168–69, 172
shut-off 26, 29, 78, 89, 117, 130–31, 168–69
storing water 116–17, 123
Whakaari/White Island eruption, 2019 8, 18, 52–53
wheelchair users 25
wildfires 18, 57–58, 76
safe zone examples 58
what to do during a wildfire 58–59
window coverage and repair during storms 39, 42
windows, broken 166
workplace emergency supply kit 101